CHILDREN AS CHANGE MAKERS

EMERALD STUDIES IN CHILD CENTRED PRACTICE

Series Editor: Sam Frankel, Learning Allowed, UK

Emerald Studies in Child Centred Practice: Voice, Collaboration and Change seeks to reposition the place of childhood studies as a discipline, highlighting its social value. This series explores the application of theories from childhood studies in practice. It highlights the place, purpose and power of these theories to inform practice and seek to shape a child-centred approach across the settings within which children live and experience their everyday lives – schools, families, the law, the care system. Uniquely, books in the series will not only draw on academic insight but also include the perspectives of both practitioners and children. The series makes the case for the need for a shared dialogue as a foundation for re-imagining practice.

This new series offers a new and valuable dimension to childhood studies with relevance for how the wider society comes to engage with it. Indeed, it offers a chance for childhood studies to increase its presence in society – to demonstrate how an awareness of children's agency and the constructed nature of society can positively influence discourse and debate – with the hope that this can increasingly shape policy and practice and add value to children's everyday experiences. Proposals are welcome for the series that align to this goal and help us to develop and grow childhood studies. The series is particularly keen to explore multifaceted aspects of children's lives, such as schooling, home lives, children's rights, child protection, activism and more.

CHILDREN AS CHANGE MAKERS

A Resource to Enhance Child Centred Practice and Extend Active Learning Opportunities

BY

SAM FRANKEL
Learning Allowed, UK

And

DANIELLA BENDO
King's University College, Western University, Canada

United Kingdom – North America – Japan – India
Malaysia – China

Emerald Publishing Limited
Emerald Publishing, Floor 5, Northspring, 21-23 Wellington Street, Leeds LS1 4DL

First edition 2024

British Library Cataloguing in Publication Data
A catalogue record for this book is available from the British Library

ISBN: 978-1-80262-714-5 (Print)
ISBN: 978-1-80262-713-8 (Online)
ISBN: 978-1-80262-715-2 (Epub)
ISBN: 978-1-80262-716-9 (Paperback)

Printed and bound by CPI Group (UK) Ltd, Croydon, CR0 4YY

This book is dedicated to our families.

To the Frankel family – as always thank you for your patience, understanding and inspiration – as you remind me on a daily basis of the power of children's voices and how we [as adults] need you [and all children] to be Change Makers.
To the Bendo family – and to my husband Steve; thank you for always making me feel like I can be the Change I want to see and for continuously supporting my desire to engage in Change Making.

This book is also dedicated to the Honourable Landon Pearson (1930–2023) who dedicated her life to advocating with and for children and their rights. Thank you for always inspiring and supporting young people in many capacities, to make a difference in the world.
'Children and youth are experts in their own lives and if we are to find workable solutions to the challenges that confront them, we need to find them together'. – Landon Pearson, 2012

CONTENTS

LIST OF FIGURES AND TABLES

Figures

Tables

FOREWORD

As I write, it feels like the world is on fire. Strife explodes in many corners of the globe… Foreboding surrounds dire changes in weather…In liberal democracies, we face an increasing erosion of trust in virtually all institutions meant to hold the promise of the economic and political system.

And then there are the world's children. Living in incredibly different circumstances. Some who can engage with their rights but many who cannot. Thousands upon thousands of children looking at the sky for bombs rather than for sunshine. Thousands upon thousands hoping for, not expecting, a good meal for the day. Yet children, in all their diversity, have at least this in common…Their parents, their communities, their countries, their faiths and their cultures would hold that they are precious.

The book you are about to read is, in my mind, an urgent call to action. Think of our world as a kite. A kite taken by the wind. Careening this way and that, with every gust, wildly out of control. Children have the ability to be the string to that kite. To hold that kite to the ground and guide it.

They cannot do this without the intentional and active support of adults who touch their lives. In terms of rights, children have the 'right to participate', and adults in every country of the world are the 'duty bearers' of this right. This means that adults have the obligation to ensure that children can meaningfully participate in the decisions that affect them. Imagine how taut and firm that string to the world's kite would be if adults chose to focus on listening to children more than they did. How might this shape decisions – such as initiating a war?

Listening to children's voices is possible because, wherever you sit reading this book, I know you have been taught that children are precious. Just by being precious, children can influence and change the adults in their world. 'Influence' to a change maker is an important form of change. Influence is a change in a way of thinking, and isn't this the key factor in what we might call 'fundamental change'?

I remember as the Child Advocate for my Province in Canada, I had the opportunity to sit with a group of 8-year-old First Nation children in their community called Wikwemikong. The community, like many in Canada, was suffering under the yoke of history and colonialism, including residential schools. I sat with the children as they described their community to me and what they saw…Until at one point, one of the little girls spoke up, 'excuse me', she said, 'I think you don't need to worry about us. You need to worry about the teenagers, because kids like us, we aren't old enough to know we have no hope'.

Boom!

Years later, I can picture and hear that little girl. Her comment has stayed with me and keeps me stopped dead in my tracks each time I remember her forcing me to reflect. She was a change maker. I will hold her comment in my memory for the rest of my life.

It is absolutely certain that children can practically impact the world.

Paolo Freire, the great educator from Brazil talked about the 'oppressed' as being rendered 'objects' not 'subjects' in the world. He argued that it was the process of 'voice' and 'agency' that gave human beings their humanity. Janusz Korczak, the Father of children's rights, wrote that 'children are people today, not people tomorrow'. Upon these, and so many great thinkers, rests this book. It is a call to action.

We all must support children in participating in their own lives, in their own communities, in their own countries and in their own world. In order for this to happen, we must cease to understand children as property, as objects, but understand them as human beings, as subjects.

We must learn to approach the world with 'love'. I use the word 'love' because I am thinking about how a 15-year-old told me once, she knew her counsellor cared about her. 'My counsellor is curious about me' she said, 'and I think it takes a lot of humility for adults to be curious. Humility, that does not come easily to you all'.

We can all be humble and curious. I believe it is within us. I'm thinking that to find those qualities, we will have to follow the lead of children, who by nature are both humble and curious.

So, read this book. As an Indigenous writer, Thomas King might say, 'You can reflect upon it. You can write a response. Send the authors a letter or an email. You can give it to a friend or colleague. You can do nothing. But, you can never live your life again as if you have never read the book. You have read it now'.

Irwin Elman
Officer of the Order Of Canada

Senior Fellow, Laidlaw Foundation
President, Defence for Children International Canada
Senior Global Advisor, Save Ukraine (Kyiv)
Strategic Advisor, Abrar Mental health and Trauma Services

ACKNOWLEDGEMENTS

This book evolved from our experiences of practice as we have engaged with children, young people, students, parents and professionals. As a result, these ideas have been shaped by many people – and to all of those who have engaged with openness and enthusiasm (when things have worked and when they have not), we say thank you.

It is important to thank our colleagues and students at King's University College. The Childhood and Youth Studies Department has created a space for creativity and innovation, and we are grateful to have benefitted from that.

We want to thank Sam's team at Learning Allowed – in particular Caroline Whalley for her mentorship and encouragement. It has been fantastic to look back on previous projects and use those to fuel some of our thinking here – so thanks to the old Act 4 team and to John Fowler.

Thank you to the team at Emerald for their patience. We got there in the end!

A special thank you to Kayla Getty, who has been working away in the background to help us pull the manuscript together. Kayla, you have been amazing!

We want to thank Irwin Elman. I *(Daniella)* remember messaging Irwin on Facebook when I was doing my Master's in 2014 to tell him that my project would focus on the Canadian Council of Child and Youth Advocates. He responded immediately with support and encouragement and invited me to come visit his office in Toronto. His support enabled me to bring my project to *life*. From this day, Irwin has become a friend and supporter, and for this, I will always be thankful. Irwin – you are an inspiration to so many, and we are grateful for your contribution.

I *(Sam)* remember taking a group of students to Toronto to support Irwin at a time when the provincial government decided to remove funding from his work as Child and Youth Advocate. It was hard to understand. Irwin's work had been transformative. It sparked a fire in me and in many of those students to ensure children's voices remained a priority. His passion has been such an encouragement to us on this project, and we thank him for providing a foreword and hope that in some small way, what we are doing here might add to the foundations he laid in Ontario – with benefits to children around the world.

Finally, Daniella…thank you for your resilience as we have made our way through this project and for your willingness to listen to my crazier ideas and help in finding ways to express them. From an ambition shared a long time ago – we have managed to get it down on paper – and hopefully this book can fuel more opportunities for children and adults to make a positive difference. Thank you!

And last but certainly not least, Sam…thank you for including me on this project and for sharing your crazy ideas with me! Your leadership and ability to dream big is inspirational, and there's no doubt it's why we were able to pull this project together. You are a *Change Maker* – and through this book, I hope we can support others to engage as *Change Makers* too.

PART 1

1

INTRODUCING THE CHANGE MAKER

'How can I make a difference'?

This book is our response to this question, one that we have both heard repeatedly from children in schools and community settings, undergraduate students who are working towards a career with young people and adult practitioners.

We are writing this book to inspire you, as adults, to:

Part 1: advance your thinking – by reflecting on and revisiting the way you see children as participants.

Part 2: increase your confidence – by engaging with guidance, practical examples and activities to strengthen collaborative opportunities with children.

PRESENTING THE CHANGE MAKER

We recognise that certain terms can carry different meanings to different people. Thus, we aim to present our view of a *Change Maker* here at the beginning, offering a foundation upon which the rest of the text builds.

> *'Change Maker' is a sense of identity.*
>
> *It is a way to think about ourselves as free to access and maximise opportunities that are meaningful in shaping how we view our participation; contributing to positive change(s) in our communities (micro or macro).*

It is a definition that centres around how we make sense of ourselves and form (and re-form) our identities. How we think about ourselves and how we come to think about others influence actions and frames experiences. Identity reflects (1) the view we hold of ourselves but also (2) how that view alternates and is (3) shaped by others and the spaces we are in (Jenkins, 2004). In short, identity formation and re-formation are a constant part of our day to day, informing our actions and reactions (what we do and what we don't do). Consequently, we assume multiple identities as we position ourselves in the varied settings and interactions that form part of daily life. Within the context of participation, this sense of identity then serves as a filter for:

- how we interpret the actions/inactions of others towards us.

- how we make sense of our acts/inactions towards others.[1]

Our exploration of the *Change Maker* centres on the relationship between how we see ourselves (our identities) and what we do (our participative engagement). We acknowledge there may be children who do not want to engage in 'change' and we are not seeking to responsibilise these children. Rather, we are opening up a space to unpack possibilities to explore the freedom we (both children and adults) have to be a *Change Maker*. As a result, we have framed three guiding statements to direct our journey:

(1) Our [children and adults] identity as a Change Maker is informed by how connected we feel to the social world around us.

(2) Our sense of identity as a Change Maker has implications for the meaning we attach to our participation.

(3) Our sense of identity as a Change Maker expands with an awareness of our own personal capabilities – freeing us to access and maximise meaningful opportunities.

Before we move on to unpack these statements, we want to highlight an observation that is worth mentioning. There seems to be a perception that children 12+ years old can engage as *Change Makers*, but not children under this age due to an assumed lack of competency. We have noticed that young children under the age of 12 years frequently want to be included and engaged but are often silenced because they are deemed 'too young'. We disagree that young children lack competency, and we believe that they too can engage as *Change Makers*. As a result, the messages that we present in this book are unique for various reasons, but especially because they are relevant to young children (as well as children over the age of 12 years old). Below we begin to unpack our notions about children as *Change Makers.*

Statement 1 – Our Identity as a Change Maker Is Informed by How Connected We Feel to the Social World Around Us

A driving force throughout this text is an ambition to create a paradigm shift that repositions how we view children's capacity as participants. This is necessary because socially constructed ways of thinking about the child have limited or restricted how we see the role of children in society (both in terms of how some children may see themselves but also, how they are often seen by adults). We mark this in Chapter 2, by contrasting two competing perceptions of participation characterised by the *Muted Citizen* and the *Change Maker.* We explore the landscape for children's social engagement, looking at some of the narratives that constrain children's participation, as well as those that can enable it. By exploring these images of children within society, alongside the motivation we have as adults for enabling children's involvement, we start to get a sense of how children experience opportunities. What becomes clear is that these experiences remain constrained by dominant assumptions, which requires a change in perspective, a paradigm shift, if they are to be unlocked.

This focus, captured in Fig. 1, illustrates the connection between societal attitudes towards children and learning and how this affects individual identity. Having explored this in a separate text, Learning Allowed (Frankel & Whalley, 2023) which we will return to below, we realised how the same principle could be applied in relation to participation, see Fig. 2. This continuum, therefore, seemed to offer a useful illustration to help us highlight the fluidity associated with participation, impacted by the context we find ourselves in (both the people we are with and the spaces we are in).

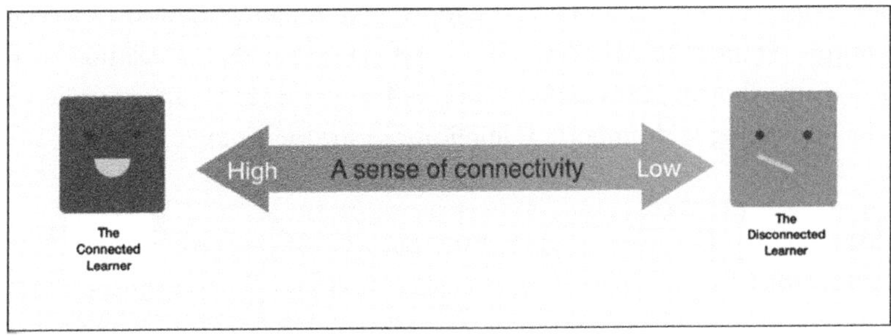

Source: Frankel and Whalley (2023).

Fig. 1. Connected Learner Continuum.

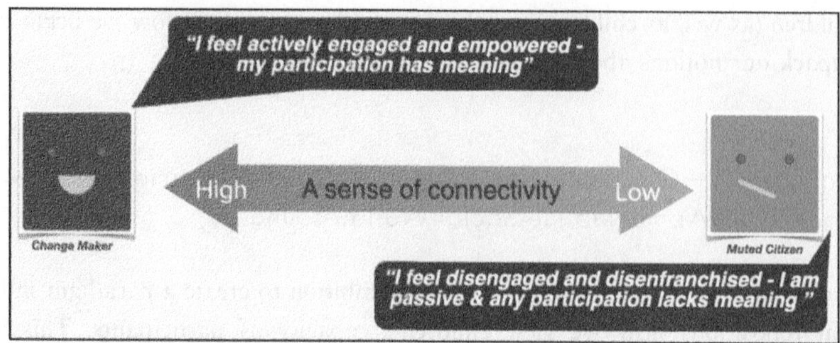

Fig. 2. Participatory Continuum.

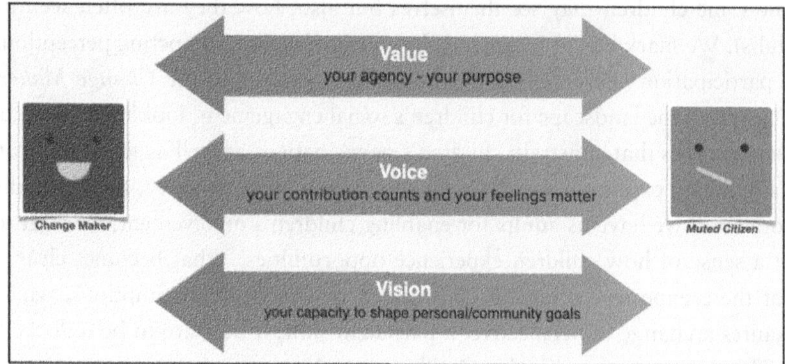

Source: See Frankel and Whalley (2023).

Fig. 3. Value, Voice, Vision.

Although our focus in Chapter 2 is on the landscape from which we define our sense of connection, and therefore, our levels of engagement, it forms the foundation for a greater exploration of the continuum in Chapter 4 as we increasingly think about those elements (internal and external) that shape meaning making. We use *value, voice* and *vision*, see Fig. 3, as a prism to help make sense of social connection. Here we take thinking applied to learning identities (Frankel & Whalley, 2023) and reflect on this in relation to the participant, showing how *value, voice* and *vision* adds to an assessment of meaning making with important implications for the *Change Maker.*

Statement 2 – Our Sense of Identity as a Change Maker Has Implications for the Meaning We Attach to Our Participation

The evolution of perspectives, over a number of years, on children's participation and their rights demonstrate the dynamic shifts in the emphasis that has been placed on the child as a participant. Notably, a major change has been a shift in adult ownership of what participation is and what it means to an acceptance that participation is meaningful to children in their own right. This chapter reviews these developments and asks how/where (and if) our view of the *Change Maker* (as defined in Chapter 1 and explored through our three statements) fits in. This highlights the change narrative around participation and how that has interlinked with an understanding of children's rights.

We further outline three key models of participation (Hart (1992), Shier (2001), and Lundy's (2007) models), including their evolution and how they are useful. However, we also address what is missing within debates about children's participation, emphasising the importance of practical application that is relevant to their lives. We explain how a re-conceptualisation of children as change makers (in the way we define it) can further enhance understanding about participation and possibilities. This chapter highlights the importance of children's identities and how they can impact opportunities for participation/change-making.

Statement 3 – Our Sense of Identity as a Change Maker Expands With an Awareness of Our Own Personal Capabilities – Freeing Us to Access *and Maximise* Meaningful Opportunities

Being a *Change Maker* does not require us to pass an exam or reach a certain stage in our life journey, but it does require us to recognise our potential as participants. Through equipping individual children to expand their own capabilities, it creates a freedom to exploit and expand opportunities to practise 'change making'. To drive this, it is important that children are in touch with knowledge of the capabilities they can bring to a social encounter. We acknowledge that various social lines of difference will impact the opportunities that children have, but the goal here is to focus on awareness around personal capabilities as a starting point.

Recognising the variety of characteristics and skills which contribute to an individual's sense of identity, our focus here centres on four key capabilities. These capabilities are valuable in extending how we view the freedom to 'be' *Change Makers*. Through extending an awareness of these capabilities, it enables (1) the individual to more freely reflect on themselves as a *Change Maker* as they respond to the social context that forms part of their everyday lives and (2) strengthens a focus for those who might facilitate changemaking opportunities.

Our four capabilities, as set out in Fig. 4 and described below are as follows:

(1) *Being a Learner*: the ability to manage, make sense and take control of a learning journey – as the individual connects with their *value, voice,* and *vision*.

(2) *Being a Pathfinder*: a knowledge creator, passionate about researching and designing ways to explore/share knowledge and understanding – instigating, collaborating, and facilitating innovative expressions of our everyday lives.

(3) *Being an Influencer*: a deep awareness and practical 'know how' to communicate and share their knowledge. This includes an understanding of different platforms for amplifying a message, as well as skills to express, explain, and listen to ideas and opinions.

(4) *Being a Connecter*: Relationships are key to change. Being able to read others and use this as a basis to frame an interaction/encounter is key to being a *Change Maker*. Pathfinder skills allow knowledge to be gathered, the 'connector' can then assess that knowledge, empathise with it, and seek to make connections that result in change.

This is summarised here in Table 1. We will come back to this a number of times in coming chapters.

Through highlighting the capabilities discussed above, within the context of the changeable way in which we form, present and re-form our sense of identity, our aim is to increasingly unlock freedom for children to explore what it means to be a *Change Maker* in their communities, maximising the

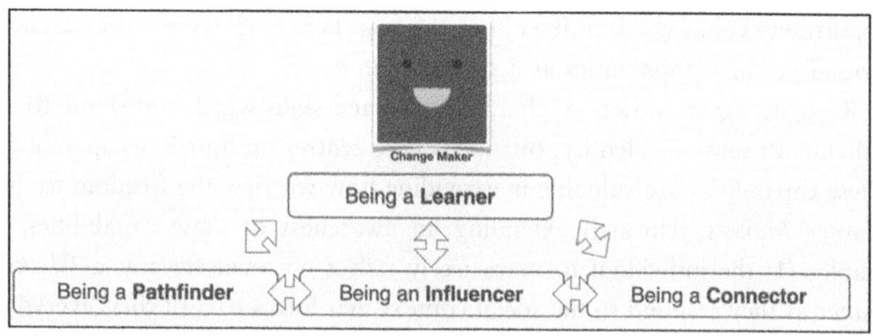

Fig. 4. Capabilities.

Table 1. Change Maker Capabilities.

	Capabilities	Attributes
Change Maker	Be a Learner	I can make sense, manage and take control of a learning journey
		I can connect with a sense of value, voice and vision
	Be a Pathfinder	I am a knowledge creator
		I know how to design research
		I am confident in asking questions and capturing and making sense of the answers
	Be an Influencer	I have a deep awareness and practical 'know how' to communicate and share knowledge
		I understand different platforms for amplifying a message
		I recognise skills to express, explain, and listen to ideas and opinions
	Be Connectors	We can recognise our own feelings and the feelings of others
		We can navigate interactions/encounters effectively

opportunities they are part of. This entails recognising the diverse interpretations, expressions, and meanings which correspond to the unique contexts and moments of our individual lives.

These capabilities are intended to offer a springboard for examining participation and the opportunities that are provided to enable engagement. We recognise the value in being open to a variety of capabilities (beyond those listed here) and to their particular relevance for children in a multitude of contexts. However, our focus on capabilities, as set out in Chapter 4, is intended to start conversations for exploring the *Change Maker* as we think about the nature of the experiences that we as adults inevitably shape.

Reflection

Through these statements, we hope that all children (and adults too) can visualise the *Change Maker* as an option in how they see themselves within their communities.

- How relevant are these statements to your experiences (a) personally and (b) whilst engaging with children?

THE NEED FOR CHANGE MAKERS

The world is wrestling with a series of existential threats. The scope of these is captured in the United Nations (UN) Sustainable Development Goals and its targets for 2030, which as we write, the world is far from achieving (for more see, UN, 2024). How we come to interact with these challenges, alongside rising authoritarianism and the invasive use of digital technology, demands (in the words of the UN Secretary General) a need for cohesion, a 'coming together' as we unite behind a 'common good' (UN News, 2024). It is with reference to that 'common good' that we are compelled to ask about the place of children to influence and shape this narrative. History (recent and not so recent) does not provide a framework for including children in such discussions. This leaves a simple question:

How are we to respond to these challenges without including children?

Children must be part of shaping that understanding of a 'common good'. For that to happen, children (including young children) need to know that they have a part to play and are welcomed, as relevant and necessary, to shaping this narrative and being part of subsequent solutions, as they desire.

In Learning Allowed (Frankel & Whalley, 2023) (which in many ways is a prequel and companion to this text), we seek to enfranchise the *Connected Learner*, breaking the bonds that have for too long restricted the way we come to see ourselves and our relationships to learning. It is a story about power over the way in which the individual is free to recognise their capacity as a meaning maker. It highlights the institutionalisation of a system of control where children's competencies are reflected in their future worth. At the heart of this approach to education, there is a wrestling match over 'knowledge'. Dominant developmental understandings of children (see Chapter 2) inform what 'knowledge' we are introduced to and when. A contemporary example might include lessons on sex, gender and relationships, which extends into accessing literature and a never-ending battle over online spaces (Financial Times, 2023). In this model, learning is something done to the child – they are 'taught to become' whatever it is that adult society prescribes. Notably, these experiences concerning learning and the access of knowledge play a pivotal role in shaping an individual's identity, resulting in deep and entrenched perceptions of ourselves as learners. These challenges carry implications for our resilience, motivation, well-being, and of course, our capacity to manage knowledge.

Why is this important? Central to those Sustainable Development Goals which we noted above, Goal 4 speaks to the need to 'ensure inclusive and equitable quality education and promote lifelong learning opportunities for all' (UN, 2024). A response to this, as seen by governments around the world, are policy decisions that re-prioritise skills around the 'processes' of learning. It shows a growing awareness and acceptance that if we are going to be able to respond to the changing nature of our world in relation to challenges from climate change to an ageing population, then we need to 'learn' our way through (Frankel & Whalley, 2023). The lifelong learner thus becomes key to any local or global solution. It invites us to reflect on the raison d'etre – the purpose of – the education system. For if the focus is on simply maintaining the status quo as it has been, then a model in which we are 'taught to become' fits, despite leading to potentially catastrophic outcomes. However, if we are interested in giving ourselves a chance, then the education system must be about something more – it must enable the individual to 'learn to be' – establishing a lifelong connection to our ability as learners. In this version of a model for education, there is an important shift, which is key to the progressing arguments in this book. For what a 'learn to be' model emphasises is not the passivity of the learner, constrained by age-based assumptions held by adults but rather the capacity of the learner as a 'meaning maker'. It reflects streams of multi-disciplinary research that get us to a point where 'learning is creating knowledge by making sense of our experiences' (Frankel & Whalley, 2023).

This is a very powerful statement that fundamentally repositions the learner in the learning process. Learning is not something that can be done for the individual, rather it is something the individual does for themselves; it is something that they are and are always doing! The nature of the opportunities that the individual is able to access and the way in which they are able to participate adds to that process of learning and knowledge creation. It creates a model where we:

- Establish ourselves as a *Connected Learner*.

- Advance our capabilities through being a *Change Maker*.

An ambition here is that the *Change Maker* becomes an active focus through which children and those that learn alongside them (parents, teachers and more) can maximise opportunities that deepen the learning experience, impacting on how we value the role we play as knowledge seekers/holders/ creators.

An education revolution (as called for by Ken Robinson, 2006, 2010, 2015) demands recognising the 'Change Maker'. It focuses greater attention on children's role as knowledge creators and how that impacts their capacity as meaning makers and therefore participants. Within environments that right-fully are required to be inclusive, it becomes increasingly difficult to justify excluding children from essential conversations about the world we live in. Being a citizen is not a static process, but one that reflects a sharing of values:

> *Social cohesion requires that all citizens share a basic common status…sense of belonging…civic pride…participation in common concerns…inclusion is not merely a right or status, but something which is actively performed.*
>
> *(Levitas, 2005, p. 45)*

It is a realisation of the place of the individual that becomes significant.

> *If a just society requires a strong sense of community, it must first cultivate in citizens a concern for the whole, a dedication to the 'common good' (Sandel, 2010, p. 7). But this 'common good' is not prescribed but rather it is co-produced:*

> *'To achieve a just society, we have to reason together about the meaning of the good life, and create a public culture hospitable to the disagreement that will inevitably arise.'*
>
> *(Sandel, 2010, p. 7 - cited in Bacon & Frankel, 2014, p. 25)*

The *Change Maker* makes this opportunity for engagement a focus of attention. It invites not only the chance to value the voice of the individual child but also emphasises the role that voice plays in shaping a sense of the common good, one that must embrace a diversity of views that reflects a societal commitment to the learner (in its broadest sense). Indeed, children's citizenship has been conceptualised as a learning process (Jans, 2004) where the journey of adults and children continually converge and diverge.

> *Through their social participation and involvement both children and adults give meaning to their actions, decide how to act and how to live their lives. Through their actions and social relationships they intervene in and shape their environment.*
>
> *(Bacon & Frankel, 2014, p. 28)*

It is on a foundation in which both adults and children recognise that they are both beings (can make a meaningful contemporary contribution) and becomings (are still learning and developing knowledge, impacting a sense of self and others) and that 'conversations' allow a collaborative response to navigating a changing world.

> **Reflection**
>
> In a rapidly changing local, national and international environment, it is our position that this sense of being a *Change Maker* is not only needed, but critical to being able to respond effectively to the challenges we face.
>
> - What and where do you see those challenges being most acute for children?
>
> - How and in what ways might the statements discussed earlier be used to focus a response to the challenges we face on a local, national or international level?
>
> - How might the three statements discussed earlier be of value and why?

CREATING A CONTEXT FOR CHANGE

To bring about a vision that sees children involved in shaping a common good we need a paradigm shift. A paradigm shift is a change in thinking; an altered mindset. In scientific terms, it marks a revision in the fundamental building blocks on which knowledge comes to be created, offering a new lens through which to look at an area of study, unveiling insights that had previously been invisible. A former colleague always used to explain the mind shift relating to a new paradigm through the use of images such as Thomas Kuhn's duck-rabbit image, see Fig. 5 (Kuhn, 1962).

The figure lures you into acknowledging the presence of one object, distracting you from seeing the other. A quick glance and… a rabbit is staring out. It is clear, obvious! But when encouraged to look again, and then again, you start to notice that the ears could be seen as a beak and then perhaps the eye, rather than facing one way for the rabbit, is facing another way for – yes – a duck! Once you see it, you wonder how you never noticed it before.

For children, the traditional and defining paradigm has centred on what children 'lack'. Our attitudes towards the child are channelled through this viewpoint, it is what we see! The consequence is that our mindset leads our actions and defines our interactions with children. It has an impact on:

Source: McManus et al. (2010).

Fig. 5. Thomas Kuhn's Duck-Rabbit.

(1) How we define participatory acts – the opportunities we create.

(2) Who is recognised as a participant – impacting identity formation and our
     sense of social connection

Alongside a growing body of scholarship in the late 1970s was a call for a
new paradigm in how we saw the child. If we looked at children differently,
would we actually be able to notice more and understand better? A feature of
the movement towards a new paradigm for children was a desire to release a
muted group from the social chains that had limited their place in society.
Early proponents of the need for this shift, highlighted the constraining nature
of social structure that was built on the propagation of the perceived ability of
one social group by another.

This came to inform the Coalescing of a range of studies into an approach that
originally was presented as a 'new paradigm for the sociology of childhood'
(James & Prout, 1990). James & Prout's argument required us to recognise the
way in which 'dominant and dominating accounts' had such an influential impact
on children's lives. They established how, for example, developmental
approaches (that drew on psychological thinking – such as the work of Jean
Piaget) became subsumed into a range of institutional thinking (from health care
to education). They challenged the uncritical way in which understandings

represented in psychological models had come to inform sociology, character-ising children as 'immature, irrational, incompetent, asocial' (Mackay, 1973, p. 28), with particular implications for our ability to both engage with and examine the 'social aspects of personhood' (James & Prout, 1990, p. 13). It was this misdirection that meant that our ability to consider children's everyday lives remained clouded, the dominance and pervasiveness of these ideas restricted how we saw the child. Society required a 'new paradigm', enacted through us being:

(1) Critical of the way in which childhood has been used to position children in social institutions shaping policy and practice (homes, schools, and community settings).

(2) Consistent in recognising children in terms of their capacity as meaning makers – social agents who are actively involved in shaping the world around them.

Despite this work being over 30 years old and the 'new paradigm' being accepted in many areas, our ambition here is to re-invigorate it as a necessary dimension in a continuing effort to position children as social participants. Jon Alexander and Ariane Conrad (2022) in their book 'Citizens' speak passionately about 'paradigm shifts'. Although not writing with a focus on children, Alexander and Conrad talk of paradigm shifts in the context of changing the story and offering a new narrative to understand the place people hold in society (2022). This, of course, is directly relevant to the goals of this book – so how do you change a paradigm? Alexander and Conrad respond by quoting from an essay by Donella Meadows:

> *In a nutshell, you keep pointing at the anomalies and failures in the old paradigm, you keep coming yourself, loudly and with assurance from the new one, and you insert people with the new paradigm in places of public visibility and power. You don't waste time with reactionaries; rather you work with active change agents and with the vast middle ground of people who are open minded.*
>
> *(Alexander & Conrad, 2022, p. 165)*

Reflecting on this quote, our job in the coming pages is to:

• Point out the old paradigm – 'we can't have a paradigm shift without a paradigm to shift to' (Alexander & Conrad, 2022, pp. 167–168).

• Powerfully advocate for the value of a new paradigm.

- Enable you (people of 'public visibility and power') to recognise how you can enact this shift.

- Create opportunities to show children as active agents of change, evidencing the positive impact of a paradigm shift.

> **Reflection**
>
> Where and in what ways are you aware of the need for a paradigm shift in children's lives?
> What impact could this have and why is that important?

HOW TO USE THIS BOOK

As we noted earlier, this book is in many ways a companion to a recent publication 'Learning Allowed' (Frankel & Whalley, 2023). 'Learning Allowed' offered a basis for reflecting on our capacity as learners (no matter who we are or where we are). It offered an assessment of the *Connected Learner* that resounded to their capacity as a meaning maker, where learning is defined by how we 'create knowledge by making sense of our experiences'. The problem, however, is that too many of us don't recognise ourselves as meaning makers, impacting the way we see ourselves as learners. Learning becomes something we do at certain times and in certain places (usually while we are younger at school). Being disconnected from ourselves as learners means that we are not as open or as aware of the opportunities for learning that are around us throughout our everyday lives.

This assessment of the learner segue into our exploration here of children as participants. How we see ourselves as participants has many correlations to how we see ourselves as learners. Being a participant is often related to certain actions in certain spaces with certain people. Consequently, our identity as a participant is limited or partial as we question the worth of our contribution (both from our own perspective but also how it will be seen by others). Using the model set out in *Learning Allowed*, we will examine what shapes how we see ourselves as participants, as we build on the *Connected Learner*.

To explore the *Change Maker* the book is written in two parts. Part 1 introduces our thinking and Part 2 illustrates our thinking in practice.

We hope that Part 2 can become a guide to support you in running your own *Change Maker* initiatives. This content will also offer examples that can be used by adults to discuss and explore effective practice.

Part 2 will be further supported by resources available on www.learningallowed.org

This glossary – Table 2 – below outlines key terms used throughout the book:

Table 2. Glossary of Key Terms.

Agency/The Social Agent	Capacity of the Individual to Make Meanings that Inform Their Actions
Capabilities	Are the learnt knowledge, skills and strategies to maximise an opportunity
Change Maker	A sense of identity. It is a way to think about ourselves as free to access opportunities that are meaningful in shaping how we view our participation; contributing to positive change(s) in our communities (micro or macro)
Competencies	A reflection on ability that is not limited by ages and stages but reflects experience
Muted Citizen	A young person (in this context) who is silenced, ignored, controlled or governed
Paradigm Shift	A big change in how we think about or understand something - a new way of seeing the world that changes olds ideas (about children/childhood in this context)
Participation	Getting involved, sharing thoughts and taking part in decisions and activities
Rights	Inherent entitlements/freedoms that we all have
Social Construction	How groups of people create and decide on ideas, rules and meanings together
United Nations Convention on the Rights of the Child	A human rights treaty that outlines children's rights up until the age of 18
UN SDGs	The United Nations Sustainable Development Goals - A set of global goals designed to address world-issues to make the world a better place
Value	Your agency, your purpose
Voice	Your contribution counts and your feelings matter
Vision	Your capacity to shape personal/community goals

CONCLUSION

The idea of this book is to merge theory with practice. We want to offer a foundation for change that invites all of us to reflect on our capabilities to participate. Obviously, we are passionate about unlocking the role that children can play in society. We recognise their energy and creativity, as well as their perspectives and insights. Change, whether that be micro (small alterations in their everyday lives) or macro (impacting the lives of many others), depends upon children being involved in the solutions. This demands a change in mindset, as we look to deconstruct attitudes and assumptions that pervade our communities. We believe a 'new paradigm' is possible. Are we being ambitious? Absolutely. Indeed, it is this ambition we are inviting you to be a part of over the coming chapters, as collectively we look for ways to inspire the power of children as *Change Makers*.

NOTE

1.   For more information see James (1993).

2

ESTABLISHING CONNECTIONS

Chapter 1 set out the following three statements:

(1) *Our [children and adults] identity as a Change Maker is informed by how connected we feel to the social world around us.*

(2) Our sense of identity as a Change Maker has implications for the meaning we attach to our participation.

(3) Our sense of identity as a Change Maker expands with an awareness of our own personal capabilities, freeing us to access and maximise meaningful opportunities.

In this chapter, we look to create a context for examining our sense of connection to the social world around us and how that influences and shapes our sense of being a 'participant' (Statement 1). As such, we set out the landscape for children's (and adult) participation through reflecting on two opposing characterisations – the *Change Maker* and the *Muted Citizen*.

Reviewing these characterisations allows us to draw attention to the social forces that continue to shape assumptions about how we see children as participants. These attitudes, that in many cases have become embedded in the social institutions (for example, home, school, healthcare and the justice system) that adults and children share, become influential in how an individual views their connectivity (which will be a greater theme in Chapter 4). What emerges, here, are the ongoing limitations and barriers that continue to frame children's participation. A call for a *paradigm shift* within Childhood Studies (see Chapter 1) to move beyond such attitudes is not new, and we acknowledge that in our use of the phrase here. However, it seems abundantly clear that despite progress in certain areas, meaningful and effective participation remains limited by prevailing societal assumptions about children. Therefore, we advocate for a renewed effort to challenge such thinking and overcome these entrenched perspectives.

The image of a *Change Maker* and *Muted Citizen* forms part of our ambitions to renew a paradigm shift in our collective thinking on children and participation. Echoing arguments from Chapter 1; if we are to establish a common good that is truly 'common', then society needs to shift the way it thinks about children. What emerges in this chapter is not only a review of the need for a paradigm shift but a more detailed examination of the landscape within which participation comes to be practised. We will, therefore, get to reflect on those pervasive views that continue to impact children's engagement, as well as begin to explore thinking that enables participation and lays the foundation for identifying as a *Change Maker*.

A PARTICIPATORY CONTINUUM

Rather than talking about a paradigm shift in abstract ways, we want, as encouraged in Chapter 1, to display a visible and practical model to enable a shift to happen. For us, that shift is most clearly marked by (1) an awareness of the *Muted Citizen* (the would-be participant), limited and restricted by those dominant assumptions that pervade societal thinking about children, and (2) increased opportunities for the *Change Maker* to actively explore what it means to be a participant. Reflecting on both the *Muted Citizen* and the *Change Maker* is best understood in terms of a continuum that marks the shift from one paradigm to another, recognising the reality that where we are on that continuum is fluid.

For the Individual Child - Perceiving Their Participatory Identity

The day-to-day reality for the individual is that we are never just the *Muted Citizen* or the *Change Maker*; rather, we will oscillate between them as we respond to a range of factors such as who we are with, where we are and what we are doing or considering to do.

Viewing our participation in relation to the continuum encourages us to recognise

- The multiple identities we and others display.

- That our identities are fluid.

- Our perceptions of self alter as a response to people, place and opportunity.

- Our sense of identity informs our meaning making, framing the way we act or react.

The fluidity of our participative identity, as we fluctuate between the *Muted Citizen* and *Change Maker*, demands that we recognise the agentic nature of the individual, their capacity as meaning makers and the extent to which the individual is impacted by social factors (Frankel, 2017).[1] These include

- How we see ourselves as similar or different from others.

- How we fit in or desire to fit in.

- Where we and others are positioned in a 'perceived' social hierarchy.

- The socially attributed value attached to certain actions/behaviours or goals.

Individually and collectively, these factors influence both how we see ourselves and how we come to see others. In short, they act as ingredients for the identities that we take on, driving our actions or reactions, with direct implications for how we see ourselves as participants! If one lacks a sense of self-worth, feels their voice doesn't count and does not believe that they can shape the social world around them, they are more likely to attach themselves to discourses that relate to the *Muted Citizen* – participation is a risk with limited value or purpose. On the other hand, an awareness of one's place and purpose means that the child (or indeed an adult) is better placed to see participation and their role as a participant in a very different light, where engagement sits alongside meaning and affirmation.

Giving visibility to both the *Muted Citizen* and the *Change Maker* allows the individual to reflect on how they position themselves in light of those different contextual factors within the myriad of social encounters they find themselves in. How the individual views themselves will of course be shaped by how they perceive they are seen by others.

For the Adult/Society – Perceiving Children's Participatory Identity

If we are to make sense of the individual's sense of identity in relation to participation, then we need to be able to explore the where, how and why that impacts their place on the continuum. The model below invites us to think about some of the layers of thinking that influence adult attitudes towards the child, ultimately impacting on children's sense of identity.

How adults position children and how this impacts on how children position themselves are presented here as an active reflection (Frankel, 2018) that can help us as adults intentionally play our part in enabling a shift in attitudes. With this in mind, imagine a paradigm shift that invites us to

(1) Be aware of the wider noise or discourses about children in society.

(2) Recognise how that is subsumed into the institutional make up of social spaces we share with children.

(3) Acknowledge how that influences the image or view of the child we hold.

(4) Accept that this image of the child will inform our practices (what we do/ how we do it and why) with children.

(5) That those practices will impact children's experiences.

(1) Children's lives are lived within social contexts that are influenced by a variety of 'noise' about the child. These are represented by the following features:

  • Constitutional/International rights – human rights.

  • Government policy – for example, the age children can vote.

  • Customs and traditions.

  • Formal practice – the delivery of healthcare/education.

  • Popular trends.

  • Legacy.

Each in its way generates 'noise' – ways of thinking about the child for example, 'moral panics'. A moral panic recognises the link between an event, news coverage, popular sentiment and policy interventions. In relation to children, moral panics reflect an awakening of misplaced assumptions that come to dominate the debate (Muncie, 2015). This leads to particular ways of thinking about the child, with implications for practice and of course, children's experiences (see 'threat' later in this chapter).

(2) Noise is transmitted in different ways and with varying emphases into the social spaces that we share with children.

Certain spaces will be open to particular noise above others – take a school and a home. A school will be shaped by the way children are presented in governing documents, national curricula and safeguarding approaches, in contrast to a home where customs, traditions and popular trends may be more influential in shaping attitudes.

(3) What we hear and how we hear it will be informed by the experiences and opportunities that we have (from the way we are parented to any professional training we undertake). All of this has an impact on the 'image' of the child that we come to hold.

That socially constructed image forms part of our attitude towards children. It is reflected in our individual approach to the child and adds to institutional understandings.

(4) These attitudes travel with us; they might change between spaces, but they offer an undercurrent of thinking that then comes to drive our motivations towards children and the practices that we seek to employ. Motivations that we have identified elsewhere include

Protection, Provision, Profit and Participation.

(Frankel, 2018, p. 61)

Notably, attitudes shaped by a traditional paradigm drive motivations that lead to actions that centre on the protection and provision (and often profit) of the child. It reflects adult centric goals, framed by a sense that the 'adult knows best'.

We are not arguing against protection and provision, but what we are suggesting is that if our motivations and, therefore, our actions are driven by 'participation', then this can lead to more effective protection and provision.[2] A new paradigm that centres on a different emphasis around participation can result in different actions and improved outcomes.

(5) Whatever those actions are, they will shape the experience the child has. This will inform their sense of identity and as a result, the 'part' they are able to play.

The paradigm we hold ultimately shapes children's attitudes towards both participation and their sense of self as a participant.
Reflecting on the *Muted Citizen* and *Change Makers* will

a. Make visible the ingredients of the old paradigm.

b. Highlight the components that encourage the need for a shift in attitude.

    c. Illustrate the landscape within which we are forming our sense of identity as a participant.

To structure this, our review of the *Muted Citizen* and *Change Maker* will consider

- What is the *image* of the child that informs these perspectives (what noise or discourses do they reflect)?

- How does our *motivation* (defined by the image we hold) shape how we 'practice' participation?

- What is the child's *experience* as a 'participant' (as a result of these factors)?

INTRODUCING THE MUTED CITIZEN

The *Muted Citizen* represents a view of the child participant that is the product of a current paradigm that continues to limit or restrict children's participation. We recognise that progress has been made in certain areas and for certain children (this will be a feature of Chapter 3), but the reality is that for most children, their experiences of being a participant are defined by (1) adult direction, (2) single or numbered opportunities and (3) activities that are place and age specific. These factors can be particularly defining for young people in challenging circumstances.

Our aim in characterising the *Muted Citizen* is to increase visibility around those dominant attitudes in society, which are such a defining feature in shaping children's experiences of participation in their daily lives.

The Image of Children and Participation – The Muted Citizen

Society is full of discourses or certain ways of thinking about the child (see our discussion on 'noise' earlier). These discourses can be regarded as building blocks that inform the image we hold of the child. For example,

Discourses: Children are Innocent.

Image: The Vulnerable Child.

Practice: Helicopter Parenting.

Children's Experience: Excessive surveillance.

Certain discourses are dominant, with deep roots in both popular thinking but also in the fabric of our social institutions. These discourses impact how we see children as participants and indeed how children see themselves.

Discourses that might impact our thinking of children as participants include ideas such as

- Children are a universal group.

- Children are in need of protection.

- Children's value is in their future worth.

- Children pose a threat to social harmony.

- Children can be moulded by a process of socialisation.

- Children lack competence (this develops with age).[3]

The *Muted Citizen* draws on these and other discourses, resigning the child to the status of passive observer, who lacks the ability to participate meaningfully. To help explore the place of these discourses in shaping attitudes, we have chosen three dominant themes: (1) children's lack, (2) the threat they pose and (3) their passivity.

Lack

Children's participation is limited due to their 'lack' of competence.

The *Muted Citizen* is born out of a defining characteristic – 'lack'. Children's relationship with adults as participants can in many ways be summed up by this one word. As such, it is unsurprising that 'lack' has come to influence the notions of citizenship and the wider relationship that has been created between children and participation (particularly highlighted in western/global north traditions). In simple terms, biological and psychological development suggests that it is with *age* that the individual grows in competence. An assessment of our capacity to reason has thus become an easy marker between the child and the adult, the becoming and the being and the observer and active participant. Children as 'becomings' defined by their lack encapsulates a wider power struggle marked by the control and management of participative opportunities. The right to vote provides an example. Its history shows the battles that has been fought to move beyond assumptions of 'lack' in relation to both women and those from ethnic minorities. The case for change drew attention to the way in which de-competencing a certain social group simply enabled the power of those already at the top (Wollstonecraft, 1792). It is a similar set of arguments that relate to ambitions for children under 18 to take part in the popular vote.[4]

For children, age has been that marker through which access has been controlled (McNamee, 2016). Efforts to free children from the dominant medical model that pervades Western/Global North constructions of childhood demand we move beyond a simple and universal understanding of the child, age and competence.[5] Rather, we are suggesting that competence is increasingly seen in terms of being 'a matter of experience - degree and not kind' (James, 1993). *The reality, however, remains that in our human desire to categorise, it is far easier to keep 'children' in a single box, where our understanding of one reflects our understanding of all.* The result is that discourses on children's lack are relied on as a core principle for 'effective' service delivery in education, healthcare, law and many other areas of children's lives.

> **Reflection**
>
> 'Lack' is an assumption that has been consistently used to frame understandings of children and participation. There are many examples where children challenge these assumptions, for example children as carers/activists.
>
> What examples can you think of?

Threat

Children pose a threat and therefore any participation must be controlled.

Are children a threat to social harmony? It is a question that has been asked repeatedly for millennia. The quotes below stretch almost 3,000 years, starting with Hesiod in around 700BC, then Socrates in 480s BC, Shakespeare in around 1610 and finally, wording from a report from the British Medical Association in 1961. *See if you can match the date to the quote* (answers are in the footnote).[6]

Dates:

Hesiod 700 BC
Socrates 480s BC
Shakespeare 1610
British Medical Association 1961

Quote A: Looked at in his worst light the adolescent can take on an alarming aspect: he has learnt no definite moral standards from his parents, is contemptuous of the law, easily bored.

Quote B: The young of today love luxury. They have bad manners, they scoff at authority and lack respect for their elders. Children nowadays are real tyrants, they no longer stand up when their elders come into a room where they are sitting, they contradict their parents, chat together in the presence of adults, eat gluttonously and tyrannise their children.

Quote C: I wish there were no age between 16 and 23, or if there were, people would sleep through it, because what happens during this time is men getting women with child, upsetting old people, stealing, and fighting.

Quote D: There is no future for society if it is to depend on the frivolous youth of today, for certainly all youths are reckless beyond words.

Ensuing a narrative about the threat children pose plays into a power hierarchy, giving those at the top reasons to establish practices that control and constrain. An unsurprising consequence is the extent to which this contributes to how we perceive children's place as participants (and how they see themselves), further fuelling an image of the *Muted Citizen*.

Geoffrey Pearson's (1983) historical analysis of 'gangs' in England highlights the ways in which this battle for 'control' has been fought through demonising children and young people over a long period of time. It plays off deeper historical ties to children as 'evil', rooted in Puritan thinking around original sin. As such, we have a mix of discourses that frame this threat, where fears over the destabilising of social harmony sit alongside the need to ensure that children are controlled and constrained. The role of the press has been an important factor in allowing this perspective of the child to be heard. A cycle emerges of (1) disproportionate news reporting, (2) a rise in popular concern and (3) leading to political action. Stanley Cohen captures this in his term 'moral panic' (Cohen, 1999). It highlights the role of the press as the mouthpiece for communicating with the public at large. Stories of 'threat' are appealing to many and as a result, help to sell papers. This, in turn, reinforces those attitudes towards the social group 'in focus' (in our case, children). It has been argued that moral panics are 'one of the most effective ways for securing policies' (McRobbie, 1994, p. 198), which suggests a level of intention within the creation of a moral panic, as those in power profit at the sake of another. An example that illustrates the extent to which such thinking impacts broader understandings of children's participation (or sense of being a participant) was 'asbomania' which impacted the UK at the turn of the millennium. Asbomania was a campaign against antisocial behaviour and marked a crackdown on teen gatherings within communities (Squires, 2008). Not only did this lead to the excessive use of legal orders to limit children's movement in communities, but it saw restrictions placed on children's clothing, as well as the increased use of products such as high-pitched alarms 'Mosquito Alarms' (only audible to children/young people) to discourage children and young people from congregating in public spaces.

It is important to note that beyond restrictions on clothing and the use of certain alarms, a more stealthy reality exists, where the increased use of surveillance ensures that young people in public spaces are constantly being watched. This raises important questions about how assumptions of young people (such as what clothes they wear through to the colour of their skin) impacts interventions (for example, stop and searches) that reinforce fears around the 'threat' that young people pose if they are not effectively supervised.[7] Notably, it is young people in disadvantaged circumstances that are commonly visible as 'threats' and who experience enhanced forms of governance and control. This all has implications for how children (from all backgrounds) come to view their role as participants.

> **Reflection**
>
> Should children's voices be controlled or enabled? Protests in schools over uniforms reflect the anxiety adults have to enable any platform for children to protest. Discuss based on the following article:
>
> https://www.cornwalllive.com/news/cornwall-news/bodmin-college-threatens-serious-consequences-8746156

Passivity

Participation is the product of children's effective exposure to social norms.

We have seen discourses reflecting 'lack' and 'threat'. Here, we consider discourses that extol children's passivity, and thus predisposition to be moulded – 'a normal child' in a 'normal' environment, can be formed into a 'normal' adult. 'Normal' here refers to the 'rule following' nature of the individual, their capacity to recognise and abide by the laws of society. It is a discourse that is firmly rooted in Durkheimian notions in which our behaviours are seen as a product of our society. Durheim was a founding father of Sociology who argued that we are the product of our society (Durkheim & Lukes, 1982). In relation to children (Parsons, 1951), this was the basis for concepts such as socialisation. Notably, socialisation doesn't really require much of the child. Instead, the process of socialisation happens around the child and is thus the responsibility of adults as they create the right contexts and opportunities so that the individual child can begin to internalise the norms and expectations of society.

Participation here is not about getting involved but about preparing the individual, through relevant exposure to (1) the 'right' environments, (2) the 'right' people and (3) the 'right' practices: supported by effective correction and reward that establishes a readiness for children to undertake their future role as members of society.

This reliance on discourses that reflect children's passivity is obvious in the way formal education establishes defined and fixed opportunities to prepare the child as a citizen. This can be seen in citizenship education, as well as in the practical nature of opportunities within school itself. School is highly controlled and structured, with implications for participation. Consider the typical school day, and the opportunities that are afforded to children to make choices or act freely (either in their interests or those of others). Children are told when to learn, what to learn and for how long. They are told when to talk, when to play, when to eat and when to take a bathroom break. Children's acceptance with the space is, to a great extent, defined by their capacity to follow these rules. Participation is, therefore, not about choice, but about following the rules, partaking in the assigned adult opportunities, and awaiting a moment when they (children) will take responsibility for structuring a future space for others to be 'educated' in the role of 'participant'.

> **Reflection**
>
> In his critique of schools, John Talor Gatto suggests that 'the truth is that schools don't really teach anything except how to obey the rules' (2005, p. 21). This creates a model of participation that is driven by achieving the 'conditional' approbation of those in authority (Kohn, 2011). The result is 'participation' is framed by asking the right questions at the right times, following instructions and doing what you're told.
>
> Is maintaining the status quo what is required to respond to the challenges of today? Discuss.

Motivations That Define Practice - The Muted Citizen

Participation is a future product of effective efforts to ensure that the needs and safety of an individual are met. Participation is thus a secondary motivation in shaping practices for children as 'Muted Citizens'.

The characteristics of the *Muted Citizen* - 'lack', 'threat' and 'passivity' (as discussed above) are pervasive, shaping attitudes and driving practices that ultimately impact children's experiences of being a participant. Internalising these discourses shapes how children see themselves, as well as how adults see them. Unfortunately, these attitudes towards children have become a 'go to' foundation for adults in framing participative engagement. As a result, adult centric motivations reflecting presumptions on the 'best interests of the child' are pervasive.

A sense of dependence, rooted in paternalism, is a foundational theme in early presentations of children's rights. Discussed in greater detail in Chapter 3, the movement that emerged was characterised by the motivation of 'saving the child', as light was shone on children's needs and the risks they face in daily life.[8] Children as 'subjects' were to be treated with special attention, as one sought to ensure their future potential and value to society. A focus on the protection and provision of the child remained at the core of developing understandings of children's rights, ensuring this continued motivation that the child had to be rescued. What this means is that 'participation' was an outcome/a product of a successful set of practices that emerged from carefully managing children as social outliers.

A consequence of being motivated by protection and provision is that it continues to undermine the value attached to children's perspectives. As such, it encourages a reliance on adult assumptions linked to those discourses discussed earlier, which in many ways simply reinforces the status quo. Take, for example, those conversations about the 'rights of the citizen', which became prominent in the middle of the 20th Century. T.H. Marshall's exposition of the citizen, focused on the civil, political and social rights bestowed by the state on certain members of society (Marshall, 1995). Such 'rights' were the gift of the state. The state in its benevolence offers the individual defined 'rights' with due warning of the responsibilities that come with them. The point being that motivation driven by provision means that those in power choose what the rights are, who is eligible and what the contract for use should include. As such, participation is framed around the formal relationship of the individual to the 'rights' provided by the state. Those who are not yet eligible remain the focus of overt supervision and educational direction until they are deemed ready to 'participate' in ways that society has defined.

'Participation' is based on status, which ensures that those who are yet to qualify remain muted, subject to a paternalistic model where understandings of participation are distorted by dominant assumptions. How we see participative opportunities is thus as preparation for a future moment and time. Until then, the individual remains subject to an assessment by others (typically adults) as to what is in their 'best interests'.

> **Reflection**
>
> Compare and contrast spaces where you have worked with children. What would you define as the motivation in that space – protection, provision, profit or participation?

Children Experiencing Participation – The Muted Citizen

So, what is the consequence of this image of children as a *Muted Citizen* constructed with narratives that reduce children to a sense of lack, threat and passivity? How, when sat alongside 'motivation' that is ordered by the role the child is expected to play in the future, does this impact their experience of participation?

To help us understand this we are going to share a case study.

Case Studies – Children and School Strikes/Political Action

How much do we really want to hear from children – let alone respond to their calls for change?

School strikes are increasingly 'in vogue', given global credence through the Fridays for Futures movement. The premise of the strike is simple – we (children) have no faith that if we simply come and speak to you (adults), you will listen; therefore, we disrupt an activity that you value as a way of highlighting an issue that is important to us, driving a conversation that we hope will lead to more progressive and collaborative action and behaviours.

The place of strikes highlights immediately the 'muted' nature of the child in society. However, what is more apparent is that when we consider some specific case studies, we see the systemic thinking that continues to constrain children's voices, limiting experiences around what participation should look like. Consider the following examples:

Iraq War and a Curriculum for Citizenship

2003 - the UK government commits to a war in Iraq. There is significant dissent. School children felt so strongly that it led to an act, which at that time, was rare. As a news report documented:

This spring, in the first days of war with Iraq, the country was witness to a new kind of protest. In the most significant child led campaign for a century, school children as young as 10 walked out of their classrooms to attend what were for most, their first political demons-trations…these young people were organising and leading their own protests, leafleting at school gates, organising e-mail networks and expertly working the media. Their determination to be heard was palpable. The results were awesome (Brooks, 2003, p. 41).

School strikes took place in the US, Switzerland, Greece, Denmark, Sweden, Italy, Spain, Australia and the UK. There were mixed responses from adults - including acknowledging the sophistication of their arguments, as well as concern over the disruption.

The UK media linked the strikes to a, then, new element of the school curriculum 'citizenship classes'.[9] The narrative emphasised how such classes fuelled children's actions - giving children ideas that were 'above their station'. Schools reacted with a method long relied on - punishment - as this threat to the status quo was controlled.

'Herein lies the contradiction. On the one hand, citizenship classes encourage children and young people to show concern for the common good', to engage in 'active citizenship' and to accept the consequences of their actions; yet, on the other hand, their 'reward' for proactively articulating their concerns over a major world crisis has been, on the whole, admonishment and ridicule (Cunningham & Lavalette, 2004, p. 265).

Shannen Koostachin

14 year old Shannen Koostachin was a young Indigenous activist from Attawapiskat First Nation in Canada. In 2008, she advocated for better educational opportunities for Indigenous children, specifically fighting over three decades for a safe and proper school for her community after a diesel spill made community members sick. The school in her community was unsafe, in poor condition and lacked basic facilities; as a result, many children stopped going to school. (The Canadian Encyclopedia, 2020).

Shannen (along with other youth in the community) advocated for safe and comfy schools by using social media platforms to encourage children across the country to write letters to the government advocating for equal educational opportunities. In 2008, the government responded saying they could not fund a new school.

As a response, Shannen's class cancelled their graduation trip and used these funds to go to parliament in Ottawa to advocate for a new school. Shannen spoke to Minister Strahl and told him that her community would not stop advocating until they were promised a new school. Finally in 2012, construction for a new school started. Sadly, Shannen passed away in a car accident in May 2010. By November 2010, Shannen's Dream (a youth organisation focused on bringing awareness to funding discrepancies for Indigenous children's education) was developed. By 2015, the new school opened in Shannen's community as a result of her persistent advocacy.

Despite some efforts to create opportunities for children to advance their position as 'citizens', some adults often remain hesitant in their efforts to fully support children. The result – participation is an adult defined task that is seen to have educational value linked to an individual's future contribution. This is acceptable, but children who frame their own agendas must at best, be heavily supervised and monitored and at worst, obstructed and contained. Participation becomes an adult sanctioned act, with consequences for how adults continue to see children, but more importantly, for how children see themselves.

Reflection

The Canadian government's resistance to Shannen and her classmates showcase how young people are often muted and ignored by adults when they attempt to engage in changemaking.

- What barriers constrain children's participation?

- Why do you think this happens to young people?

- What do you think enabled Shannen and her classmates to succeed with their advocacy efforts?[10]

INTRODUCING THE CHANGE MAKER

A paradigm shift demands we recognise moving from one position to another. So, if the *Muted Citizen* characterises an existing paradigm, we now need to set out the alternative.

Above we considered discourses that represent children in terms of their 'lack', their 'threat', their 'passivity' and how those create an image of children as a *Muted Citizen*. In this section, we seek to offer an alternative perspective that centres on children's capacity as meaning makers, actively responding to the social environment that they are part of. As we will see, a change in how we see the individual has profound effects on how we view what participation is and how one might participate.

The Image of Children and Participation – The Change Maker

Children as Meaning Makers

There has always been an awkward juxtaposition between those images of the child that define the *Muted Citizen* and the characterisation of children in literature. Indeed, looking back on some widely read children's novels from the last 150 years, we see numerous examples of children putting their agency (their capacity as meaning makers) into practice from Tom Sawyer and Huckleberry Finn to the many and varied characters of Enid Blyton and Arthur Ransome and to the vivid and extraordinary Pippi Longstocking, courtesy of Astrid Lingraad through to Roahl Dahl, Jaqueline Wilson and of course J.K. Rowling's Harry Potter. These stories show children engaged in their everyday lives, empowered, through their creators as meaning makers, whose competencies are demonstrated as a response to the different opportunities that they find themselves in. The stories highlight the tension between wider social structure and the way children are able to put their capabilities into practice. In these stories, adult practices, for example ordering of the school day, regularly constrain children's ambitions, leading them to subvert the status quo as they find alternative paths to reach their goals. In the recent musical adaptation of Roahl Dahl's 'Matilda', we see this young girl searching to find her place in the world. For Matilda, her 'moment' is when she realises that she can take control of directing her own 'story' which is expressed in the lyrics to the song 'Naughty'.

Matilda represents one of a range of child characters that found their voice through a realisation of their capacity and an activation of their capabilities, enabling them to take meaningful steps that allowed them to navigate their particular lives.

'Activating' one's capacity to take control, to engage with one's potential, commonly revolves around a quest that the character 'finds' themselves on. Perhaps this is most completely demonstrated in the Harry Potter books, where it takes a series of seven novels for Harry to really understand who he is.

That journey of personal discovery, heightened in literature, is common to all of us (although this may happen at different times and to varying extents and usually without broomsticks), as we seek to know who we are and where we fit into the world. In many ways, it reflects the possibilities of a personal shift in our own mindset as we are freed from the perceptions of ourselves that relate to the *Muted Citizen*, and we start to realise our capacity as an active meaning maker, ready and able to contribute to the social spaces that we share with others.

At the centre of this is an awareness of the process of agency. As discussed in Chapter 1, it presents the individual as active in their ability to make meanings from the social context they find themselves in. This has implications for not only how they see themselves and others but also how they act or react to a given set of circumstances. Rather than children being the product of their social context, they become the creators of it (see James, 2013). Notably, there are spaces where a freedom to choose, for example, might limit how the individual expresses their agency, but they still make meanings, and those meanings will contribute to their relationship with that space, the activities and those within it.

Accepting children as social agents changes how we come to view an interaction and what it is that an interaction may achieve. Table 3 shows the contrast between the repetitive efforts to instil knowledge to prepare children for the future to a dynamic interaction space, where children and adults, as partners, create and pursue shared goals.

Table 3. Comparisons.

Image of Child	Understanding of the Child	Perception of Adult-Child Encounter
Muted citizen	Lack, threat and passivity	Static and one dimensional nature of the outcomes
Change maker	Active agent/meaning maker	Numerous possibilities

These 'possibilities' allow us to present an alternative way of viewing children's social engagement. Educationalist John Dewey (2010) in the first half of the last century expressed these possibilities by challenging traditional notions of competence, by defining children's competency as a 'potency' or 'force'. This characterisation encapsulates the shift that we are arguing, as we move from a sense of passivity to the active and power filled image of the individual child as a catalyst for change.

> **Reflection**
>
> What encourages children's participation/agency? Think about ways that adults can support children's capacities/agency/participation.

Motivations That Define Practice – The Change Maker

An image of the child that is imbued with an active recognition of children's agency shakes up those traditional motivations that we saw with the *Muted Citizen*. For if children are meaning makers, then a question such as 'what is in the best interests of the child' can only fully be answered by asking children themselves! The consequence is that issues of protection and provision can only be effectively understood and responded to through enabling children's participation.

Here, we start to explore how a shift towards participation coincides with an effort to re-position children in relation to their capabilities to be *Change Makers*. However, the reality is that creating those spaces for participation is not that simple. What stands out from a quick glance through history is the lack of space that has been provided to enable children's effective participation. These do emerge as parts of movements, where children create their own platforms to support their participation. Here are some examples:

1899 – New York children's newspaper strike.

1976 – Soweto Uprising.

2018 – March for Our Lives.

2018 – Fridays for Futures.[11]

What each of these examples shows is a tension between practices of participation and ongoing dominant attitudes that continue to reflect the *Muted Citizen*. There is a sense of deviance about the place of children on these particular platforms, as they step outside of 'normal' understandings of childhood. It makes the demonisation of the child participant easy, as reference is made to how they have gone beyond the bounds of their place within society.[12] However, even when such children are lauded, it is with reference to their exceptionality, creating an idea that only certain children can demonstrate effective 'participation'.

Participation here emerges as a willingness to subvert adult authority and the expected roles of childhood through actions that defy what it means to be a child. *This is a problem.* Not only does it limit the way adult's come to view participation but it also impacts the meaning that children give to being a participant. Our view of the *Change Maker* looks to 'normalise' participation to make it part of everyday life, where there is a shared ambition for participation between children and adults. This desire to see a shift in attitudes demands, as we have said before, an alternative. A focus on capabilities offers a focus through which participative opportunities can be re-defined, which can lead to changing practices and re-establishing relationships.

Motivated by a Desire to Extend Capabilities

In Radical Help (2018) written by Hilary Cottam, she sets out many years' worth of practice focused on making effective change in communities. Her book offers an important vision for participation. Cottam (2018) starts by challenging the need to 'help', as one responds to perceived 'needs'. Although not written with children in mind, this corresponds with that pervasive view that children need to be 'saved' (shared earlier), with implications for how we perceive children as participants. Cottam (2018), with arguments that reflect the need to move beyond a motivation that is driven by provision, explains that

> *The emphasis is not on managing need but on creating capability: on addressing both the internal feelings and the external structural realities that hold us back. (p. 15)*

A recognition of the social constraints and the limitations placed around the individual reflect findings from international development with the realisation that solutions were likely to be effective and sustained if they were generated from the 'bottom up' rather than the 'top down'. It sets out a series of arguments that illustrate the dominating colonial perspective to change, where the wealthy (Global North) 'saviour' would deliver their solution to the perceived need of a poorer (Global South) community. Those such as Paulo Friere (1970) offered an alternative that centred on valuing the individual in a community. As such, it offered a starting point to empower, where change stemmed from hearing the voices of communities and enabling them to design and lead a response.[13]

Moving beyond assumptions becomes a feature of enabling this shift as we establish a motivation for practice that is not based on 'help' but on 'empowerment'. That is not to ignore or reject the needs that groups in society have, it is rather to say that by engaging with them, our ability to understand those needs and enable effective responses, is improved. A significant part of Cottam's (2018) motivation is a recognition that rigid and limiting images surrounding certain groups have held back the effectiveness of state led interventions, for example in health and education. Notably, she highlights the 'production line' that lies at the heart of the educational experience of so many. In response, she argues

> *Modern life requires a broader range of skills, including the ability to collaborate, create and think laterally. In this century our most important skill is our ability to continually learn. (p. 32)*

It is an ambition to keep on learning, with its recognition of the active and engaged role of the individual, that offers a view of participation that is both ongoing and inclusive.

This engagement with capabilities is being recognised by childhood scholars. Larkin (2023) talk about capabilities as 'people's functioning - that is, their actual ability to do the things they value doing or being'. This links to Sen's (1999) original definition around freedom, which forms a key part of how we have interpreted the *Change Maker*. However, what this work with children has also done is show the broader social factors (as explored in relation to the *Muted Citizen* above) that impact on the way the individual can express their freedoms. In a list of five questions, Larkin (2023) invite children to reflect on the context they are in and how that shapes their ability to engage and activate their ambitions.

(1) What do you (or other children) want to be able to be, to have and to do?

(2) What helps and what gets in the way of children being able to be, have and to do these things they want?

(3) What has happened recently and in the more distant past that has created
     these things that help or that get in the way?

(4) Who and what can we work with to create more of these things that help
     and to get over the things that get in the way?

(5) How can we make sure that any improvements last?

(Larkin, 2023, p. 232)

It is through asking these questions that we not only get a sense of the
barriers but also start to get a sense of how those freedoms might be enabled.
Thomas and Stoecklin (2018) argue that in pursuit of the individual's 'freedoms or opportunities to achieve functioning' (p. 78) (those things they value),
we need to be aware of 'the resources available to children, which include
adult care and concern[…]as well as resources that support their autonomous
action' (p. 80). In exploring this they reflect on how this includes an understanding of 'the conversion factors (personal, social and environmental) that
turn those resources into capabilities' (p. 80). Such a focus reinforces the value
of examining those contextual factors that shape children's everyday lives and
how those impact on their journey as a *Change Maker*.

As we consider the *Change Maker*, this must start with a desire to look
beyond assumptions that have previously limited children's freedoms and be
motivated by the active and engaged role of children as social meaning makers,
from where we can invite them to activate their capabilities. It is a basis that
has already demonstrated important contributions to shaping practice as we
will see in Chapter 3.

Reflection

Think about what makes collaboration/participation effective. What
capabilities would you see as enabling and why?
    Discuss your ideas.

Children Experiencing Participation – The Change Maker

A shift in the image of the child as a participant not only re-frames practice it also
impacts on the nature of children's experiences and the opportunities that come to
be created. Projects such as the case study discussed below highlight the possibilities that a paradigm shift provides.[14] It invites a sense of the active role children

can play, and also, the extent to which it can impact a community – it introduces the potential of *transformation*.

Case Study

Extract from (Frankel & Whalley, 2023, p. 20)

A research initiative that captures the transformational impact that children's voices can have on communities, including how they are seen as learners, was a project called the The Shinning Recorders of Zisize in South Africa (Children Count). What was so powerful about this research was the way it allowed the researchers to not only question but to present to the wider community, the power hierarchies and assumptions that framed how children were positioned within society. Through giving the children a microphone and inviting them to start conversations with adults in their lives about issues that were relevant to them, adults began to hear children differently. One example, was an interview that 10-year-old Mpumelelo conducted with his mother following the selling of his goat. Mpumelelo explains that after a day away from the family home, he got back to find the goat had gone and when 'I asked them[…]they ignored me'. When he asked his mother about this, she said 'we decided that it was better to see it and buy you another one'. In response to why he was not told, his Mum said 'it's because we felt that you were still young and we didn't think that we needed to tell you'. The brilliance of the project lay in simply enabling these conversations to happen. Through equalising the power through the use of the microphone, Mpumelelo was able to have a conversation he would not otherwise have been able to have, challenging and changing his mothers' perceptions and creating a new basis for their relationship. This was summed up by another parent who responded to an interaction with their child (on a different issue) by saying, 'I never realised that [you], my child, felt the pain of what we were going through at that time in our lives. I didn't think children were aware of so much that is going on around them' (Meintjes, 2014, p. 162). The foundation that enabling children's voices offered in relation to promoting positive change was reflected in the comments of the school principal[…]

> *What I have learnt is that we look at kids or think about kids as not being aware of issues, or of issues not affecting them. But after hearing the programs [the children's recordings] I've realised that children know about things we think they don't know about. I realised that they know, and if given the chance to speak about*

those things, they speak. I realised that they think deeply about these things and these issues that they raise…I no longer look at children as mere children who do not know anything. I look at them as people who know something and who have something to say to me, and who can speak freely and be just as confident as an adult.

(Meintjes, 2014, p. 163)

It is a compelling extract that highlights the transformational impact of giving children the chance to be part of 'the conversation' for their voices to be heard.

Reflection: How Are Children Involved and What Works Well?

Read about the following project being carried out by the Scottish Children's Parliament regarding climate change – how does this show children as *Change Makers?* How could you apply this to your practice?

https://www.childrensparliament.org.uk/our-work/learning-for-sus tainability/#LfS_Part1

CONCLUSION

Representing the continuum here acts to mark the need for open discussion around where an individual sees themselves in different spaces and at different times, as they come to assess their *value, voice* and *vision* as a foundation for effective participation. It allows us to consider how we move up and down this continuum, and as a result, we can discuss the factors that influence this for us. Simply enabling that conversation around our level of connection begins to allow the *Change Maker* to become visible, as well as casting light on some of the barriers and enablers that influence any shift.

Practical Ideas: Start a conversation using the continuum (Fig. 6), think about:

- How or why is the continuum helpful?
- What does the continuum offer?

Note: This is developed further in Part 2.

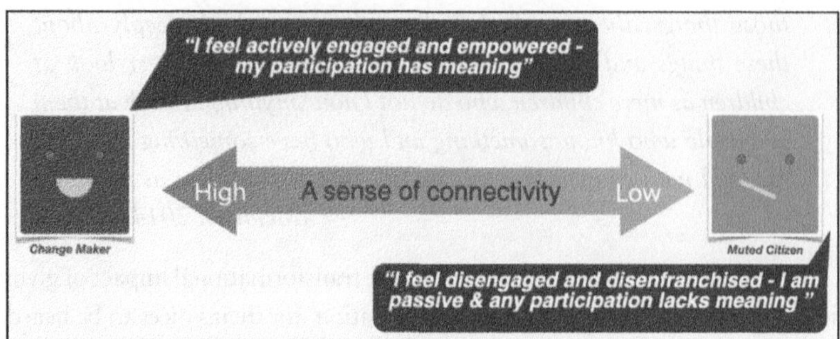

Fig. 6. Participatory Continuum – Repeated.

NOTES

1.   A definition of agency that we have used elsewhere highlights the contextual and relational nature of the meaning making process – [agency is] 'contextually mediated capacity of the individual to make meanings that inform their actions, that are relationally situated and morally constituted and which are framed within a range of elements that make up children's personal lives' (Frankel, 2017, p. 97).

2.   For example, see Kitzinger's (1997) work on child abuse.

3.   These discourses are explored in more detail in (Corsaro, 2017; McNamee, 2016).

4.   For more information, check out John Wall's (2021) book: Give Children the Vote.

5.   Childhood Studies textbooks offer an overview of this, see (McNamee, 2016; Wyness, 2019).

6.   Quote 1 – 1961 - Pearson, 1983, p. 17. Quote 2 - 480s BC - Brake, 1980, p. 1. Quote 3 - 1610 - Shakespeare, 1970, p. 337. Quote 4 - 700s BC - Cote, 1994, p. xi.

7.   An interesting example is the introduction of technology in school uniforms in China as a means to supervise children (Telegraph, 18/12/2018).

8.   For more see Cunningham (2006) and a discussion around 'rescuing children' during the Victorian era.

9.   Introduced as part of curriculum changes in England and Wales in 1998.

10.   For more, see The Indigenous Foundation:
https://www.theindigenousfoundation.org/articles/the-legacy-of-shannen-koos-tachin-and-shannens-dream
First Nations Child and Family Caring Society:
https://fncaringsociety.com/shannens-dream-learn-more

11.   To find out more about these see the links below:
https://www.zinnedproject.org/news/tdih/newsboys-strike/
https://www.sahistory.org.za/article/june-16-soweto-youth-uprising
https://marchforourlives.org/
https://fridaysforfuture.org/

12.   For example, the documented attitude of the then US President Donald Trump's towards youth activist Greta Thunberg, see https://www.theguardian.com/environment/2019/dec/12/donald-trump-greta-thunberg-time-magazine

https://www.cnn.com/2019/12/12/politics/greta-thunberg-donald-trump/
index.html
https://www.cnn.com/2019/12/12/politics/trump-greta-thunberg-time-person-of-
the-year/index.html
13.   See more information in Freire (1970) and White (1996).
14.   For more on discussions around participation and transformation, see
(Frankel 2023a, 2023b; Percy-Smith et al., 2023; Tisdall et al., 2014).

3

REFLECTING ON IDENTITY

Chapter 3 invites us to explore the second of our three statements

(1) Our [children and adults] identity as a Change Maker is informed by how connected we feel to the social world around us.

(2) *Our sense of identity as a Change Maker has implications for the meaning we attach to our participation.*

(3) Our sense of identity as a Change Maker expands with an awareness of our own personal capabilities, freeing us to access and maximise meaningful opportunities.

This takes us on a journey through different participatory frameworks, which we recognise emerge from within a very particular context framed by the children's rights agenda.

This chapter, therefore, offers an alternative mode of thinking where we are required to engage with the extended meanings that form part of a participatory encounter, as we look at how meaningful and authentic an opportunity proves to be. Driven by a reflection of the capabilities the individual perceives to access social opportunities, it moves participation on from being systematic (step by step) to recognising understandings of its unstructured nature relating to the individual context that shapes our everyday lives. *A key part of this thinking is a recognition of the messiness of participation.* Opportunities are not definable, repeatable or universal; rather, they are messy, fluid and individual. In order to showcase this, we compare and contrast participation models to our participation continuum outlining those points of convergence and divergence.

In profiling this chapter, it seemed necessary to track the journey of key milestones relating to children's rights and participation developments/models that have emerged over time. As a result, we have created a timeline of these key historical milestones that are outlined below. This chapter seeks to review these developments and ask how/where (and if) our view of the *Change Maker* (as defined in Chapter 1 and explored through our three statements) fits in. This will allow us to review the *Change Maker* in the context of current discourses on children's rights. Rights remain essential to our ability to position children within participative approaches. Rights remain the international language; therefore, if we are thinking about any sense of the common good, they must form part of any exploration.

Arguably as a response to the way in which children's rights have developed, a separate and more specific language/discourse has arisen around participation. This in many ways reflects limitations with 'rights' and the need for the individual to increasingly be given an element of agency within the activation of their choices/actions. By examining approaches to participation alongside our statements on the *Change Maker*, we see new avenues to re-envision how participation and rights are thought about to spark opportunities for change-making.

PARTICIPATION AND RIGHTS

The children's rights movement has had a rich history in terms of its developments and the impact it has had on shaping discourses about childhood, community/NGO work focused on children, and on legislation that pertains to young people's lives. Notably, this has established a backdrop within which our understanding of participation has developed - with implications for both adults (how we come to view what participation is) and for children (how they view being a participant). Particular milestones throughout this history have sparked these developments, which are important to outline below because they show a shift in terms of how children/childhood were thought about and also lead to key discourses and understandings that we know and use today. In order to understand these discourses, we start by first outlining these key historical developments.

Children's Rights Movement: The Timeline of Key Events and Developments

19th century – The 19th century marked the beginning of the Children's Rights Movement as policies and legislation began to develop for the first time, in an attempt to protect and enhance the lives of children.

1909 – Ellen Key (1909) published *The Century of the Child* (Thorne, 2009) which outlined the need to re-conceptualise understandings about childhood in the Westernised world. Ellen Key played a major role in the cutting-edge shift in thinking about children and the saving of childhood (Thorne, 2009).

> *After World War I and later WWII: collateral damage had affected young people immensely which drew attention to the need for child protection measures and the ongoing commitment to compulsory schooling.*
> *(Cordero Acre, 2012; Marshall, 1999; Polonko & Lombardo, 2015)*

1919 – the International Labour Organisation abolished child labour to eliminate hazardous working conditions for children (Arce, 2012; Ennew, 2000; Fass, 2011).

1924 – the League of Nations agreed to protect children's rights under the Declaration of Geneva. Eglantyne Jebb in 1924 founded the International Save the Children Union. It became the first NGO to support young people after the war and developed the first draft of the Declaration of the Rights of the Child (Ennew, 2000). Although it never became part of international law, it high-lighted the importance of protecting young people and established a basis for children's rights (Doek, 2009; Fass, 2011; Marshall, 1999).

1948 – the adoption of the *Universal Declaration of Human Rights* (UDHR) served as the first time nation-states agreed to set out fundamental rights and freedoms for all human beings in international law (Arce, 2012; Ennew, 2000; Fass, 2011).

1959 – The UDHR set the framework for human rights which led to the adoption of the Declaration of the Rights of the Child in 1959 (Ennew, 2000; Marshall, 1999).

The International Covenant on Civil and Political Rights and the International Covenant on Economic, Social, and Cultural Rights stemmed from the UDHR and offered human beings the legal protection of human rights (Pare, 2017).

1960 – The UN developed the United Nations Emergency Fund (UNICEF) to focus on the protection of children and their rights internationally.

1979 – The International Year of the Child signed by UN Secretary General to bring awareness to issues impacting young people internationally.

1989 – The Convention on the Rights of the Child is adopted which outlines fundamental human rights for all children; it becomes the most widely ratified human rights treaty in history.

1990 – Adoption of the African Charter on the Rights and Welfare of the Child.

2000 – The African Movement of Working Children and Youth and the Latino-American Movement of Working Children and Adolescents.

2000 – The Optional Protocol on the sale of children, child prostitution, and child pornography is adopted to further enhance children's protection rights.

2015 – The Sustainable Development Goals are adopted.

Ongoing: developments focus on the promotion of children's participation, protection and provision rights.

These historical developments are milestones because they fundamentally changed that way children were thought about in relation to participation. For instance, they put the spotlight on children's well-being and recognised the importance of prioritising and supporting children. Yet, carefully reviewing these milestones showcase a set of childhood discourses that are rooted in legal understandings about children. For instance, we see the following key constructions that emerged as a result of these events:

- The child in need of protection/the vulnerable child. As a result of dangers associated with war, it led to a new commitment to protecting children from harm (Arce, 2012; Reynaert et al., 2009) and shifted children's social position as rights-holders (Jans, 2004).

- The rights-bearing individual child, equal, and universal rights for all children. This viewpoint leads to an understanding of children as sites of intervention/individual entitlements for all children (Freeman, 2007; Hanson & Vandaele, 2003; Wyness, 2013).

- The universal child, based on universalised rights that should apply to every child, without acknowledgement of the important role of context and social lines of difference.

- The child's right to a say, based on notions that children can have a say in decisions that impact their lives, but this is contingent on age-based capacity/competency.

As evidenced, the predominant messaging is that children need to be protected, and we as adults have a role to play in implementing children's protection. However, what's missing is the meaningful participation of young people. While there is a recognition of children's participation rights, these understandings are based on age-based notions surrounding competency. For instance, Article 12 of the UNCRC has been focused on widely due to its novel recognition of children's right to express their views. However, consider the developmental language used in the article:

> *States Parties shall assure to the child **who is capable** of forming his or her own views the right to express those views freely in all matters affecting the child, **the views of the child being given due weight in accordance with the age and maturity of the child.**
>
> (Article 12, UNCRC, 1989)*

As a result, children (especially young children), can't really be meaningfully involved in participatory processes or outcomes since they aren't included in constructing their own identities and are oftentimes treated as *Muted Citizens* who do not have agency. This perhaps stems from the fact that these understandings are rooted in legal conceptualizations based on the UNCRC. Although the UNCRC has been extremely helpful for setting a standard about children's rights internationally, as mentioned above, it has contributed to a particular conceptualisation of participation that does not fully consider children's agency. There is no doubt the UNCRC has had a positive impact on recognising and acknowledging children's participation rights; however; we want to move beyond traditional notions regarding children's participation rights and universalised notions outlined in the UNCRC, because some of these ideas are problematic and don't align with children's lived realities. Consider the following critiques linked to this international treaty:

- It ignores the cultural contexts in which children live.

- It is abstract and generalised, which makes application to local situations difficult.

- It adopts a universalised approach to children's lives and fails to account for important social lines of difference that impact children's lives, such as disability, culture, gender, and sexuality.

- There is limited accountability on governments when it's time for them to report implementation of the UNCRC and also respond to recommendations from the UN Committee on the Rights of the Child.

- It was developed over 30 years ago and as a result has not progressed to account for emerging issues impacting young people's lived realities (for example, cyberbullying and digital worlds).

By re-thinking participation in the context of the *Change Maker*, we can start to re-conceptualise how to advance notions about children's rights that move beyond legal understandings of the UNCRC. The key to the *Change Maker* is the value in a focus on relationality, which can help to not only implement children's participation rights, but accurately understand children's lived realities/experiences. As Hilary Cottam (2018) contends,

> *Relationships matter more than anything else...Emphasis should be paid to relationships, starting with the premise that everyday human connections matter and they need to be nurtured and sustained....When we start to make policy that is rooted in everyday lives, then we can make effective change.*
>
> *(Cottam, 2018)*

The notion of the *Change Maker* has a lot to do with relationships. It offers a tool to further critiques of the UNCRC (for example, that it is abstract, universalised and fails to account for gender/culture) because it acknowledges the important role that relationships play in thinking about children/childhood. This, in turn, has the potential to contribute to a new paradigm shift that focuses on children's capabilities and their abilities as a *Change Maker*. If we look at the children's rights timeline (above), it's evident that key legal instruments have set a foundation for recognising and understanding children's participation rights; but these instruments do not apply or fit perfectly in children's lives. Therefore, there is a need to move beyond any one single type of legal understanding about children's rights and/or singular participation models. Instead, it is important to ensure that there is space to make sense of any participatory encounter within specific contexts of how each individual perceives their role as a participant. This requires engaging relationally with the individual, but not just in the moment, but rather in the messiness that surrounds participation, acknowledging the range of factors that shape any ambition to 'do'/be part of 'change'.

> **Reflection**
>
> Think about the UNCRC and some of the critiques listed above. How could a focus on relationality help to better support children's participation?

COMPARING CHILD PARTICIPATION MODELS/DEBATES WITH THE PARTICIPATORY CONTINUUM

Below we have identified three prominent models of participation. Each model has been influential and offers an example of the way in which researchers have sought to move from the legalistic language around protection and provision to embrace a framework for effective participation. However, through looking at points of convergence and divergence with our notion of the *Change Maker*, we look to add an additional dimension to these models. The aim here is not to argue for one model above another, or indeed to suggest that our efforts here offer an alternative rather what we seek to encourage is a recognition of participation, not as a snapshot of one single moment or experience, but as part of how we see ourselves as we respond to the social world around us. That is, 'our sense of identity as a change maker has implications for the meaning we attach to our participation'.

The Models

Since the end of the 20th century, scholars have continued to heavily focus on children's participation in political and social contexts (Hart, 1992; Jans, 2004; Percy-Smith & Thomas, 2010; Shier, 2001; Stoeckline, 2013). Research has analysed young people's experiences with collective participation in governance, youth councils, youth parliaments, advocacy initiatives, service delivery systems and policy consultations with young people (Gal & Duramy, 2015; Jans, 2004; Lansdown, 2014; Lundy, 2018; Percy-Smith & Thomas, 2010). Yet, the concept of child participation in both theoretical and practical spheres has remained complex and controversial (Lansdown, 2014). These complexities stem from the historical constructions and emergence of various understandings/models surrounding participation that have evolved over time.

Model 1 – Hart's Ladder

Review. For instance, within the context of childhood studies, the work of Roger Hart has been a catalyst to thinking about participation. In 1992, Hart developed a ladder of children's participation, see Fig. 7 (focused on children under the age of 18) based on of Sherry Arnstein's (1969) adult participation model, which includes eight levels of participation. What Hart did was provide a measure through which adults could consider the level of engagement they were providing. Notably, in doing so Hart was starting to break down the ingredients of participation. As one of the rungs on the participation model, Hart (1992) classified *tokenism*, along with *manipulation*, as a form of non-participation in children's decision-making and referred to these concepts as instances when children's views and experiences are sought by adults but are not actually taken seriously by them. While scholars have identified strengths of the model for its effectiveness in evaluating and assessing children's participation, others have critiqued the model. For instance, scholars have pointed to the unequal and hierarchical imbalance of power between adults and children in regard to granting them participation outcomes (Kirby & Gibbs, 2006). Others have also argued that the model ignores adult's inability to enable participation for children (Kellett, 2009) and have attempted to improve it by rearranging the main components into a circle to deconstruct the hierarchy. Despite its critiques, it is widely used in organisations that service children (for example, non-profits that service children, provincial and territorial child and youth advocate offices in Canada and more).

Reflection

Looking at Hart's model in Fig. 7, think about childhood examples for each 'rung' (apply each rung to a childhood example). What 'rungs' do you like and find effective for working with children? Are there any issues with any of the rungs that you can identify? Think about how childhood is portrayed in each rung.

Convergences and Divergences. Our participation continuum (including the *Muted Citizen* and *Change Maker* from Chapters 1 and 2) is relevant to the rungs on Hart's ladder of participation. For instance, looking at rungs 1–3: These rungs do not offer child-centred or 'meaningful' forms of participation to children and are focused more so on adult-initiated decision-making.

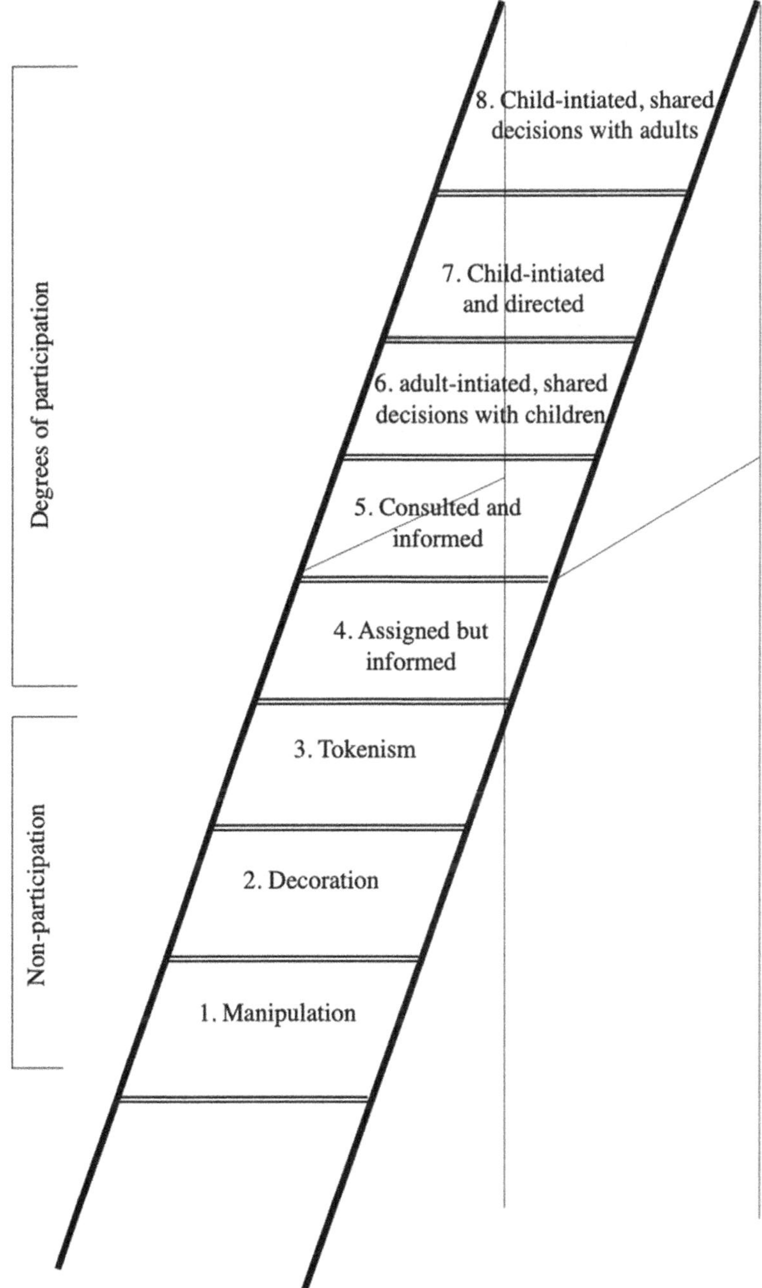

Fig. 7. Hart's Ladder.

Therefore, these rungs resonate more so with our description of the *Muted Citizen* as children are not the key decision-makers in the participatory processes or outputs. Comparably, rungs 4–6 are more so in line with a shift on the middle of the participation continuum (between the *Muted Citizen* and the *Change Maker*). For example, young people are more involved in participation processes and outputs, as they are informed and consulted on decisions and ideas, but they are not leading these decisions or processes. Lastly, rungs 7–8 align more closely on the continuum with the *Change Maker* as children have enhanced freedom to lead processes, decisions, and outputs. The *Change Maker* looks to normalise participation and to make it part of everyday life where there is a shared ambition for participation between children and adults (as outlined in Chapter 2). Rungs 7–8 start to offer this shift in viewing children as having the capabilities to freely initiate, direct and share in decision making with adults. While adults still have a role to play in rungs 7–8, there is a shift in the power dynamic between children and adult's roles in that adults are adopting more of a supportive/collaborative approach to children's ideas and agency. This shift opens possibilities for children to engage as a *Change Maker* (especially with rung 7 where children are initiating and directing participatory processes). Rung 8 is also important because children have a role to play with decision making; however, in applying our participatory continuum, differences arise in that our focus is more so on developing opportunities for young people to recognise and activate their capabilities. This is the key difference of our approach; recognising, fostering, and supporting relationships and capabilities to help spark change-making at micro and macro levels. As Cottam (2018) outlines,

> *Starting from possibility is important; this approach contrasts with twentieth-century systems that assess risk and then attempt to manage it. That perspective is destructive. It encourages us to focus on what might go wrong rather than build towards what could go right. (p. 200)*

It is 'possibility' that flows from a focus on capabilities; shifting the viewpoint from those limiting discourses of 'lack, threat and passivity' that we looked at in Chapter 2. We now turn to another participation model to assess similarities and differences with the participatory continuum.

Model 2 – Shier's Pathway

Review. In 2001, Shier offered an alternative approach to Hart's (1992) child participation model, known as pathways to participation. Shier's (2001) model, Fig. 8, outlines different levels of participation which focus on collaboration between adults and children and adult's role in granting children participation. The model encompasses three stages of commitment at each individual level: *openings, opportunities* and *obligations* that individuals and organisations can apply to promote child participation. Kirby and Gibbs (2006) have critiqued the model to highlight that initiatives and experiences cannot be attributed to one single level of participation, and decision-making powers rapidly shift depending on context. They further suggest that the model fails to identify how children engage in decision-making, and the different types of support adults can offer to account for diverse and changing experiences and differences amongst young people. For example, a child facing challenging circumstances or who may be impacted uniquely by social lines of difference may resonate with various levels of participation (not just one or the other) depending on their circumstances. Similar to Hart's model in Fig. 8, Sheir's model is widely used internationally in organisations/service-delivery systems that account for children's participation.

> **Reflection**
>
> Looking at Sheir's model below, think about childhood examples for each pathway (apply each pathway to a childhood example). What pathways do you like and find effective for working with children? Are there any issues with any of the pathways that you can identify? Think about how childhood is portrayed in the various pathways.

Convergences and Divergences. We can once again apply the participation continuum to identify convergences and divergences. For instance, this model focuses more heavily on the *Change Maker* vs the *Muted Citizen*. Most of these pathways prioritise a conception of children as active meaning makers in their own lives. This is evidenced in the attention that is paid to children's voices, listening to children, children's involvement in decision-making, and power dynamics between adults and children. On the other hand, the model is more so focused on adult's viewpoints and commitment to working with

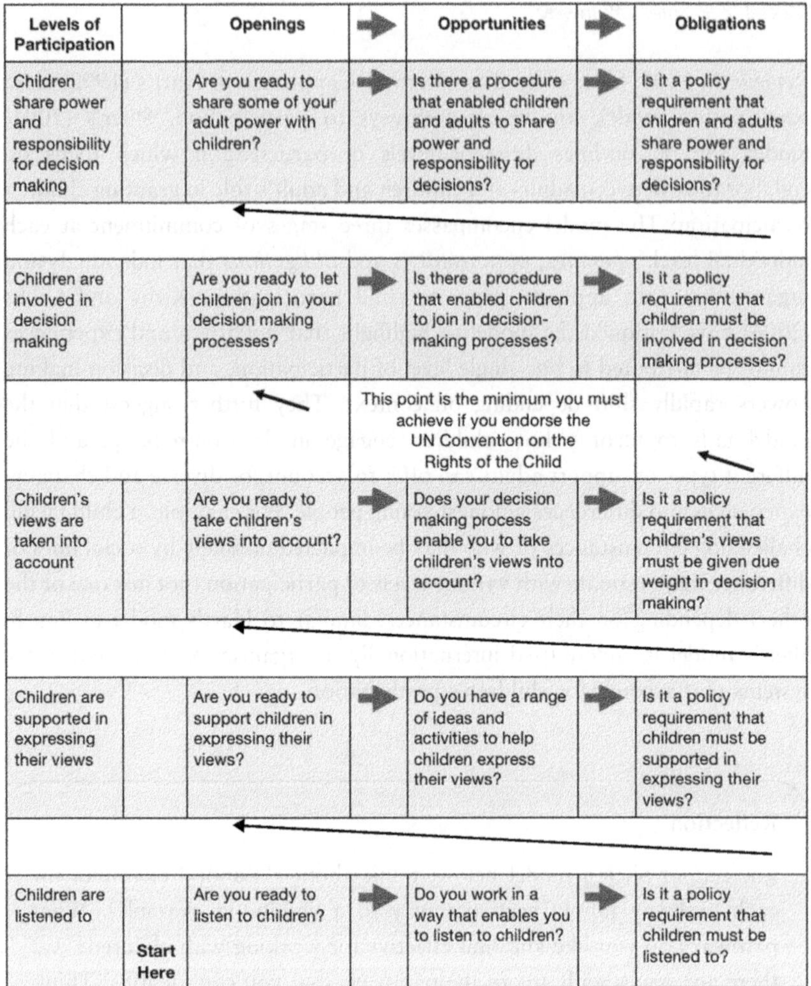

Levels of Participation		Openings		Opportunities		Obligations
Children share power and responsibility for decision making		Are you ready to share some of your adult power with children?		Is there a procedure that enabled children and adults to share power and responsibility for decisions?		Is it a policy requirement that children and adults share power and responsibility for decisions?
Children are involved in decision making		Are you ready to let children join in your decision making processes?		Is there a procedure that enabled children to join in decision-making processes?		Is it a policy requirement that children must be involved in decision making processes?
				This point is the minimum you must achieve if you endorse the UN Convention on the Rights of the Child		
Children's views are taken into account		Are you ready to take children's views into account?		Does your decision making process enable you to take children's views into account?		Is it a policy requirement that children's views must be given due weight in decision making?
Children are supported in expressing their views		Are you ready to support children in expressing their views?		Do you have a range of ideas and activities to help children express their views?		Is it a policy requirement that children must be supported in expressing their views?
Children are listened to	Start Here	Are you ready to listen to children?		Do you work in a way that enables you to listen to children?		Is it a policy requirement that children must be listened to?

Fig. 8. Shier's Model.

children, and as a result, the model is not developed for children to use/engage with. If adults respond 'no' to the various probes, they may fall more so on the left side of the continuum, towards a viewpoint of children as *Muted Citizens*. If adults respond 'yes' to the various probes, there may be additional opportunities for them to begin to recognise children as *Change Makers* by acknowledging and supporting their capabilities and creating spaces for children to engage as active meaning makers. Again, we see the importance of focusing on the recognition of relationality between children and adults, as well as a recognition of possibilities and capabilities that shape their identity as a participant – played out not just in a defined task but across the different spaces and interactions of their everyday lives. We now turn to another example of a popular model of participation to compare and contrast the participation continuum.

Model 3 – Lundy: Space, Voice, Audience, and Influence

Review. In 2007, The Lundy Model of Participation developed from confusion about practitioners' obligations regarding the understanding and implementation of Article 12 of the UNCRC. The aim of the Lundy Model of Participation (2007), see Fig. 9, was to provide a clear conceptualisation of Article 12 for practitioners working with young people in an attempt to highlight how to implement children's participation in *meaningful* ways. The four main components of the model include space, voice, audience, and influence (Kennan et al., 2018; Lundy, 2007). *Space* entails a safe and inclusive environment for young people to express themselves; *voice* includes the facilitation of young people's expressions of their perspectives; *audience* includes members or individuals who listen to young people's views; *influence* includes action based on young people's views (Lundy, 2007). While the model highlights the importance of reaching beyond the concept of voice to understand child participation, it also aims to deconstruct power imbalances between adults and children (Lundy, 2018). Numerous scholars have identified strengths of the model and its contribution to the concept of meaningful participation that entails more than just the concept of voice (Kellett, 2009; Kennan et al., 2018; Tisdall, 2008). McCafferty (2017) analysed Lundy's (2007) model to show examples of how professionals working with young people in different service delivery sectors (specifically, in child welfare) can apply these components in a way that effectively implements Article 12 of the UNCRC.

Reflection

Looking at Lundy's model of participation in Fig. 9, think about examples for each element linked to your experience of studying or working with children. What elements do you like and find effective for working with children? Are there any issues with any of the elements of the model that you can identify? Think about how childhood is portrayed in the model.

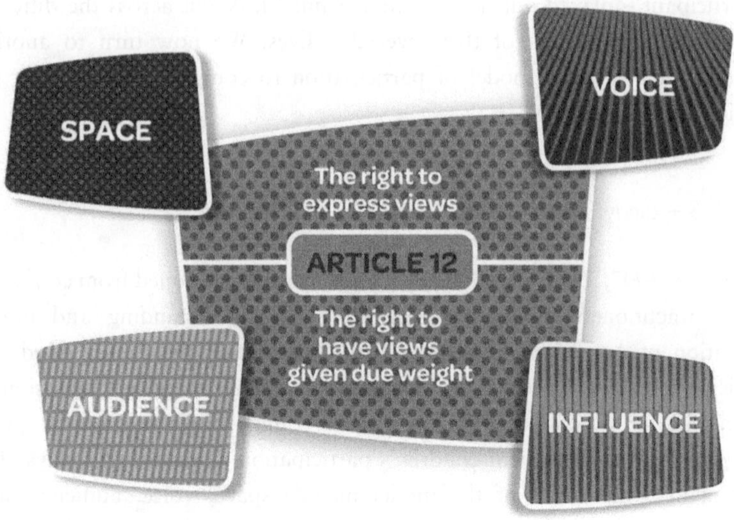

Source: Lundy (2007).

Fig. 9. Lundy's Model.

Convergences and Divergences. In applying the participation continuum, these elements of the model are all relevant to the *Change Maker*. Space, voice, audience, and influence are all important elements that can enable changemaking because there is a focus on children as active agents and on identifying participatory spaces for children and adults to work together. With Article 12 in the centre of the model, the model acknowledges children's rights to express their views, but it also adheres to the UNCRC's conceptions surrounding a child's capability to express their views (for example, if you can't express your views, then this shifts what opportunities you may have to share your ideas. Therefore, there is an understanding of capacity that is based on developmental notions). This is where the model diverges from the participation continuum. The continuum places a different emphasis on capabilities by recognising a broader interpretation of capacities through a focus that *assesses the extent to which the individual is able to exploit/maximise the opportunities within their everyday lives.* That doesn't mean we simply look at whether we are able to do what we want, but rather at the nature of the possibilities that are opened up in the context of the 'messiness' of a participative experience. This moves us away from expression as just 'voice' and puts it more firmly into an understanding of 'identity' and how this fosters various forms of participation.

Summary. Although this is not an exhaustive list of child participation models, these scholars and models highlight the complexity of participation and showcase the various understandings associated with the term. The models may be accessible and of practical use to some children, but for the most part, they focus on theoretical discussions for adults. What we are interested in is how we can complement these models through inviting adults and children to come together to explore how they apply theory and activate projects that enhance our shared understandings of participation.

RE-THINKING PARTICIPATION MODELS IN THE CONTEXT OF THE CHANGE MAKER

Reflecting on the models we have just shared, we are reminded of how important it is that as well as managing those process steps that inform a participative encounter; we are also in a position to question, review, and assess the way the individual comes to perceive themselves. That sense of identity as a participant both pre, during, and post a participative opportunity will impact on the experience, and therefore, has to be a factor in our understanding of participation and subsequent change. In presenting the *Change Maker* – what we are hoping is that this increasingly puts the child at the centre of this inquiry.

Collectively, we believe that participation should indeed be meaningful and can take many forms, but what we are really interested in is the need for the question of meaningfulness to be child-centred (rather than defining meaningful participation from an adult-centric viewpoint). To do this, we re-visit the concepts of *value*, *voice*, and *vision* (as noted in Chapter 1, see Fig. 10 below) within a participatory context.

These concepts can help to create a child-centred approach to participation.[1] What we are arguing is that as a result of children enhancing

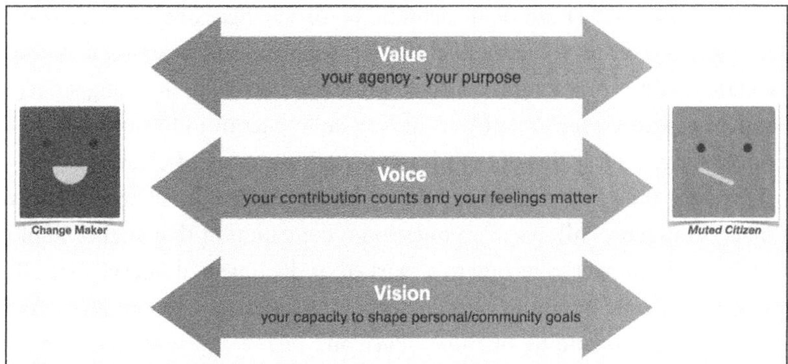

Fig. 10. Value, Voice, and Vision.

their connection through recognising that they have *value* to offer, their *voice* matters, and they have capacity to shape various personal/community goals into a *vision*, it gives children greater freedom to make choices about the nature and degree of their participatory actions or reactions. As a result 'connection' contributes to meaningfulness.

Adults notably have a role to play in supporting those levels of connection. Here relationships are key to the way in which the individual child is able to 'connect' with their value, voice and vision. It adds to a conception of participation where rather than the focus being on a set of guidelines constructed by adults, we concentrate on how children perceive themselves within their experiences, impacting on their meaning making and ultimately, the contributions they choose to make or the visions and ambitions they have.

Meaningful participation is thus impacted by the individual's connection, as assessed through *value*, *voice* and *vision*, determining

- a desire to extend their capabilities.

- their level of engagement (as they enact or do not enact, their social agency).

For this to happen, children need to be able to see themselves as *Change Makers*. Through our efforts here to bring to life the ingredients that shape the participant (the participatory continuum and the *Change Maker* capabilities), we hope to add to the extent to which the individual is able to 'do' participation.

Our viewpoint on participation stretches beyond simply participating in an initiative or event and stresses the importance of relationality and meaningful engagement as part of acknowledging the messiness of a participatory encounter. As noted above, there are barriers to child and youth participation and the various common models that are used to discuss child participation. A *Change Maker*, however, can have an impact at all levels of participation and has the potential to draw on participatory processes or initiatives to lead to an outcome: *change*. Traditional definitions of change are associated with modifying or altering something. However, we believe that change can also be associated with re-thinking a concept, gaining a new skill, inspiring someone, questioning knowledge and power, having an impact or influence on someone or something, even if this doesn't lead to 'big' instances of change.

Through their participation, the *Change Maker* has 'influence' and 'impact'. 'Influence' allows us to question a contribution that shapes thinking or ideas, with 'impact' referring to a marked or documented intervention. Both can be seen, contributing to participation, at a micro- or macro-level. As we deepen our understanding of *value, voice* and *vision* and how that informs a level of connection, we can increasingly look to understand the way this shapes levels of 'influence' and 'impact'. This is relevant both from the perspective of the *Change Maker* but also from adults who might create the space within which those levels of connection can be advanced. For example, practices that result in a presumption of the *Muted Citizen*, as reflected in case studies from Chapter 2, limit the participative experience, in contrast to settings where practices reflect and encourage the *Change Maker*.

CONCLUSION

At the start of the chapter, we highlighted our focus on Statement 2:

> *Statement 2: "Our sense of identity as a change maker has implications for the meaning we attach to our participation."*

The various models of participation that we unpacked are useful tools for thinking about connecting to the social world around us, but they may also hinder connections because they are structured and specific, and not all of these models apply to all children. To enhance these understandings, we can think beyond them to understand how we can foster connections that strengthen identities as a *Change Maker*.

Our sense of being a *Change Maker* will contribute to our levels of engagement:

- what we participate in.

- how we participate.

- what we consider participation to be.

This may also enable opportunities for participation and a recognition of the value of participation in individual contexts.

As well as considering participation in relation to models, like those we have reviewed, we are inviting children to consider the extent to which they are able to demonstrate their capabilities as part of putting their identity as a *Change Maker* into practice. It is through this everyday reflection on connection and capabilities that children are in a stronger position to practically explore what it *means* to participate. Through this, the individual will naturally restructure the social context and encounters they are a part of.

While participation models (such as the ones outlined above) remain important tools to children's engagement, our aim is to enhance these viewpoints by drawing attention to the importance of relationality, as well as children's identities and capabilities as *Change Makers*, which we outline further in Chapter 4. We believe this is a key element to enabling children's meaningful participation as a *Change Maker* because identity isn't always acknowledged in traditional models/frameworks. As we highlight above, our identities as a *Change Maker* have implications for the meaning we attach to our participation. In order to do this, we believe that we need to de-construct traditional notions associated with children's rights that have impacted childhood discourses. These viewpoints stem from legal understandings that may be well-intended but have historically prioritised children's protection over their participation. With a focus on protection (which is no-doubt important to children's health and well-being), there is not a lot of space for children's agency, voices, or engagement. In the next chapter, we take these viewpoints and start to think about how they link to the capabilities of a *Change Maker*.

Reflection

Thinking about the concept of participation, identify qualities or traits that you believe make it meaningful. Next, begin to think about the changemaker. How do these qualities or traits enable change-making?

NOTE

1.   For more on a review of child-centred practice see Frankel (2023a) - see Chapter 2 (Spencer & Thompson, 2023).

4

ACTIVATING CAPABILITIES

INTRODUCTION

(1) Our [children and adults] identity as a *Change Maker* is informed by how connected we feel to the social world around us.

(2) Our sense of identity as a *Change Maker* has implications for the meaning we attach to our participation.

(3) *Our sense of identity as a Change Maker expands with an awareness of our own personal capabilities, freeing us to access and maximise meaningful opportunities.*

Our journey so far has positioned the *Change Maker* as an alternative to the *Muted Citizen*. A key distinction has been an assessment of competence. Competence is an identifiable to open battle ground over which children's place as participants has been fought (as we have seen in previous chapters). Having recognised children's social agency in the presentation of the *Change Maker* in Chapter 2 and the importance of the relational dimension to rights and participation models in Chapter 3, here we think in more detail about the opportunities that seeing children as meaning makers creates. As such, we focus on 'capabilities' as a way to explore extending the identity of a *Change Maker* and equipping individual children to realise the role they can play as a participant.

EXPLORING THE CAPABILITIES OF A CHANGE MAKER

In Chapter 1, we defined the *Change Maker* in the following way:

> *'Change Maker' is a sense of identity. It is a way to think about ourselves as free to access and maximise opportunities that are meaningful in shaping how we view our participation; contributing to positive change(s) in our communities (micro or macro).*

It is a definition that views the child in relation to a set of 'capabilities'. Noticing 'capabilities', as we did in Chapter 2, allows us to be increasingly observant of the 'force' that children are. Consequently, it makes visible aspects of the participative process, creating a focus that enables a shift in mindset and a growing awareness of our individual ability to direct change and inform that 'common good' and a shared vision for communities.

What Amartya Sen (1999) argues in the Idea of Justice is that our perception of justice must increasingly be centred in the everyday, moving away from any sense that justice comes to be defined by the machinery of society (the law courts, social welfare provision, access to education and so on). What Sen presents is a notion of justice that uses our freedom to choose as a marker for a 'good life'. In the past, 'good' was viewed in relation to

- Economic position (economic egalitarian).

- Happiness (utilitarian).

- Personal effort (libertarian).

The result: what is justice is based on outcomes – the enjoyment of one's life and the money we have to spend (as a consequence of the machinery of social life).

For Sen (1999), however, an assessment of the 'good life', should not be restricted by outcomes, but by the ongoing choices we are able to make between 'different kinds of life' (p. 18). Whether we can make that choice or not will be determined by our capabilities (for example, Cottam (2018) illustrates the decision-making of families that had a chance to build confidence in their capabilities). Extending one's personal capabilities not only impacts on the freedom we have to make choices about our lives, but it also puts us in a position where we can contribute to the lives of others, as we 'decide how to use the freedom we have' (Sen, 1999, pp. 18–19). In valuing a person's ability to take part in the life of the society, there is an implicit valuation of the life of the society itself. This interconnectedness between the individual and their surroundings is central to the extent to which freedom and opportunities are created. Opportunities thus become less about the goals that we are able to achieve, and become more about the 'lives we manage to have' (Sen, 1999, p. 227).

If freedom and opportunity is more defined by how we manage or navigate our lives, then it requires a consideration of how that is done. Capabilities, therefore, become *a focus through which we can assess the extent to which the individual is able to access and exploit/maximise the opportunities within their everyday lives.* That doesn't mean we simply look at whether we are able to do what we want, but rather at the nature of the possibilities that are opened up.[1] As a result, we get a sense of the following:

> *The capability approach focuses on human life, and not just on some detached objects of convenience, such as incomes or commodities that a person may possess, which are often taken, especially in economic analysis, to be the main criteria of human success. Indeed, it proposes a serious departure from concentrating on the* means *of living to the* actual opportunities *of living.*
>
> *(Sen, 1999, p. 233)*

In short, a 'capability is the power to do something' (Sen, 1999, p. 19). In return, this creates an accountability that reinforces the relational dimension of the capability approach, as we recognise that our freedom is not only directly entwined with those of others, but our choices will influence the choices they too can make. It is our position that *children need to be aware of the power of their capabilities* and for this to inform how they position themselves as participants in their communities. Any paradigm shift, as set out in earlier chapters, is therefore marked by the enfranchisement of the child, as they realise their capabilities and connect that to the freedoms they have within the context of their everyday lives.

So much of how we think about children's capabilities has been dominated by developmental understandings. For instance, the idea that the older a child gets, the more competence they will acquire. The result is that the child is seen in terms of what they 'lack' - as a 'becoming'; impacting both how children see themselves and how they are seen by adults. Acknowledging the child as a social agent places value on their capacity to make a contribution to the present – they are a 'being'. It is about recognising children (and adults) as both 'beings' and 'becomings' that offer an opportunity to rethink the awareness we all have of our own capabilities! Below, we explore how that might influence changemaking.

DEFINING THE CAPABILITIES OF THE CHANGE MAKER

Chapter 2 introduced our image of the *Change Maker*. Here we seek to cast further light on capabilities and the potential this has for enhancing the active way in which an individual forms and re-forms a sense of identity as a participant.

We recognise the multiple contexts of children's lives creating a variety of childhoods. This will impact the way children think about freedom and the nature of the opportunities they can access. However, the *Change Maker* offers a starting place to begin a conversation about what those capabilities might be to enhance the choices open to children. A key part of this is that we have some sense of what we are talking about in relation to 'capabilities' as part of 'participation'.

The importance of making participation 'visible' has been noted earlier. In education, the concept of 'visible learning' (Hattie, 2009) added a dimension to an understanding of what learning involves. Through defining some of the component parts that inform how we 'learn about learning', it made different aspects of the learning process explicit and thus a focus for attention. This has enabled educators to create a focus that allows the individual to enhance an understanding of what it is that shapes the learning experience.

Participation, like learning, is a term that can in practice, be defined in different ways. Part of what we hope to achieve below is to provide a focus not just for talking, but for doing, using the capabilities we have chosen as a springboard for deepening engagement. Alexander notes the difference of 'citizen' being a noun or a verb. As a verb, acting as 'citizen' becomes about exercising 'power to determine the quality of our lives' (Alexander & Conrad, 2022). It is an important idea in terms of our focus on identity and reflects our ambition of the *Change Maker* as a role that can be assumed. Through the following capabilities, we begin to see how participation might come to be 'done' as we explore extending the opportunities and thus the choices we can make in managing our everyday lives.

Four Change Making Capabilities

Being connected as a learner is not our focus in this book (for more see Frankel & Whalley, 2023); however, 'being a learner' does remain a starting point for advancing those participative capabilities that are set out below in Fig. 11. Our capabilities thus begin with the 'learner', which is supplemented with the additional focus that comes with being a *pathfinder*, *influencer* and *connector*.

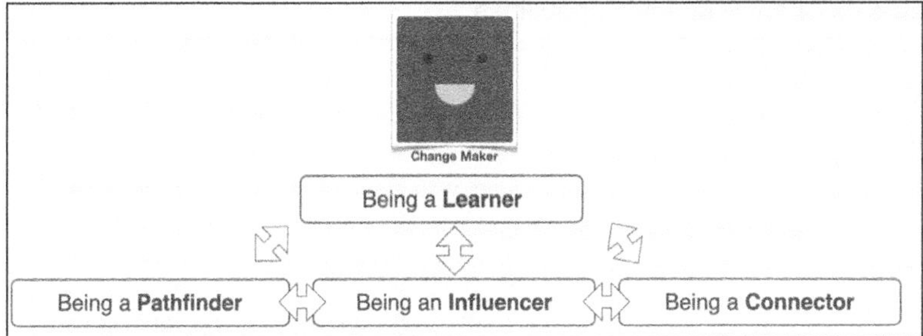

Fig. 11. Capabilities (Repeated).

Having recognised 'being a learner' as a foundation we then start to think about those capabilities that extend how the individual is able to maximise a participative opportunity. The capabilities below (which we noted are not mutually exclusive) provide an illustration of capabilities that reposition the individual within social encounters both with peers but also across generational boundaries. We also want to note that these qualities are not pre-requisites but rather are complementary characteristics that can really help to re-centre more of a child-centred approach to engagement and thus changemaking.

(1) *Being a Learner:* The ability to manage, make sense and take control of a learning journey – as the individual connects with their *value, voice* and *vision.* Seen as a vital foundation for the *Change Maker.*

(2) *Being a Pathfinder:* A knowledge creator, passionate about researching and designing ways to explore/share knowledge and understanding – instigating, collaborating and facilitating innovative expressions of our everyday lives.

(3) *Being an Influencer:* A deep awareness and practical 'know how' to communicate and share their knowledge. This includes an understanding of different platforms for amplifying a message, as well as skills to express, explain and listen to ideas and opinions.

(4) *Being a Connecter:* Relationships are key to change. Being able to read others and use this as a basis to frame an interaction/encounter is key to being a *Change Maker.* Pathfinder skills allow knowledge to be gathered; the 'connector' can then assess that knowledge, empathise with it and seek to make connections that result in change.

We have summarised this in the following table, Table 4.

Table 4. Change Maker Capabilities.

	Capabilities	Attributes
Change Maker	Be a Learner	I can make sense, manage and take control of a learning journey
		I can connect with a sense of value, voice and vision
	Be a Pathfinder	I am a knowledge creator
		I know how to design research
		I am confident in asking questions and capturing and making sense of the answers
	Be an Influencer	I have a deep awareness and practical 'know how' to communicate and share their knowledge
		I understand different platforms for amplifying a message
		I recognise skills to express, explain and listen to ideas and opinions
	Be Connectors	We can recognise our own feelings and the feeling of others
		We can navigate interactions/encounters effectively

(1) Being a Learner – A Learning Mindset Is Key to Change

Table 5. Be a Learner.

Be a Learner	
	I can make sense, manage and take control of a learning journey
	I can connect with a sense of value, voice and vision

The ability to manage, make sense and take control of a learning journey, as the individual connects with their value, voice and vision. Set out in Table 5.

Establishing one's capability as a learner becomes a foundation for the *Change Maker*. Learning here is referred to in its broadest sense. Learning is defined as 'creating knowledge by making sense of your experiences' (Watkins et al., 2000, p. 5) and as such reflects a core activity that will apply as much to the individual in a classroom as to those beyond. Here, we see the *Change Maker* as an extended learning persona, one that offers deeper and more specialised knowledge, skills, and strategies relating to community engagement and interaction.

In Chapter 1, we profiled the place of *value*, *voice* and *vision* as a tool for investigating the level of connection that an individual felt, with implications for their image as a learner. Here we build on this, recognising that an assessment of this connection forms a basis for us to expand our capabilities as *Change Makers*. As a learner, how we sense our *value*, *voice* and *vision* determines our connection and as a result our ability to 'create knowledge by making sense of our experiences'. This capacity to 'learn' is a core capability of the *Change Maker*, and as such, we share briefly what this entails.

Capabilities as a *Connected Learner* thus revolve around the individual's capacity to make sense, manage and take control of their learning, as they tune into an examination of their *value, voice* and *vision*. This narrows down to a focus on the following (for more see Frankel & Whalley, 2023):

- Individual reflexivity – acknowledge the processes of meaning making.

- Meta learning (learning about learning) awareness – recognise and can navigate the parts of the learning journey.

- Emotional expression can express feelings and emotions.

Defining these aspects of learning allows the individual (and a facilitator) insight and, as a result, gives them a level of control, impacting their sense of *value, voice* and *vision*. It is this capacity to manage a sense of one's place and purpose within a learning encounter that becomes key to the *Change Maker* effectively exploiting and maximising their opportunities. This demands that the participant, like the learner, has a sense of

Value – in who they are and their capabilities.

Voice – their contribution matters.

Vision – the freedom to make choices to further their ambitions.

Recognising what it means to be a learner creates a solid foundation for extending further, the capabilities of the *Change Maker*.

(2) Being a Pathfinder – Accessing Knowledge Is Key to Change

Table 6. Be a Pathfinder.

Be a	I am a knowledge creator
Pathfinder	I know how to design research
	I am confident in asking questions and capturing and making sense of the answers

A knowledge creator, passionate about researching and designing ways to explore/share knowledge and understanding, instigating, collaborating and facilitating innovative expressions of our everyday lives. Set out in Table 6.

We are facing some very particular challenges around access to, and the sharing and receiving (digesting), of 'knowledge'. The phenomena of 'knowledge by algorithm' sees us relying on what is in our inbox or on our media feed as the source of information. As convenient as this might be it does raise questions about whether we are simply receiving information we 'like'. How is this impacting our relationship with knowledge and assumptions? It was an awareness of the capacity to be critical that was so defining in the Enlightenment of the 18th Century – 'the enlightenment left us with a belief in the value of learning' (RSAblog).[2] Within this, a shared commitment to conversation and debate fuel a desire to understand. Are we losing that? It is a connection with knowledge and knowledge production that we highlight here.

Alderson (2017) talks about 'Utopian' research and its ability to promote justice through more effective means of 'documenting, imagining and analysing' experiences. It is an awakening of such skills that she presents as part of putting us in touch with our capacity as a 'researcher', adding to a shift through recognising our 'prophetic identities' (Alderson, 2017). Such is the importance that Alderson writes:

> *Everyday reform, therefore, depends on children being involved, education in critical questioning of present, social, economic and political repression and injustice and in creating alternative structures.(Alderson, 2017, p. 186)*

Research and the skills to question – open the door for creating a culture that changes personal mindset and organisational practice.

The 'Pathfinder' – Exploring This in Practice

As Christensen and James (2017) note, how we position children as researchers says something about:

- Perceptions of agency,

- The reach/effectiveness of global discourses on rights and

- The attitudes of those who shape spaces children inhabit.

Our 'pathfinder' draws on a variety of academic and practice-based work that has attempted to reposition children as researchers. In keeping with our ambitions to create a paradigm shift, this body of work has emphasised an emancipatory agenda. It has shown the value in projects that have sought to break down barriers surrounding knowledge as a means for establishing a more informed basis for effective change. For example, an evolving feature of these initiatives has been the recognition of children as co-participants in the research process. As a consequence, a focus has emerged on the processes that allow children not only to take part but to initiate and direct.

Case studies give us an increased awareness of what participating in research involves and the knowledge, skills and strategies that are relevant. Much of this revolves around managing power (a defining feature of a paradigm that recognises the *Muted Citizen*) and balancing this through the need for reciprocity shaped by ongoing reflexivity.

Questions such as the following offer a starting point to address some of this:

- Who conceives the project?

- Who selects the methods?

- Who does the work of finding out what needs to be found out?

- Who does the analysis?

- Who interprets the work to the outside world?

(Thomas, 2017, p. 162)

We have added to this through the format below (Frankel & Whalley, 2023), as we seek to combine not only the practical aspect, but also the reciprocal and reflective dimensions of a research encounter.

Have an idea – what are you going to investigate

What is research? Who can do research? What does it mean to be curious?

Talk and Listen – can you turn your idea into a question

What is a question? Where can you look to find out information related to your question?

Create a Plan of Action – how will you ask your question

What are research methods? How might you design a research project?

Give it a Go – put your plan into action

Interview skills, arts-based engagements and managing data

Keep on Learning – what does your data say?

Data analysis, presenting your ideas and evaluating impact

This is detailed further in Part 2.

Enabling such attributes has significant positive potential through encouraging a 'curiosity' that is 'driven by children's desire to learn more about other children and their living situations' (Liebel, 2008).

It is that sense of curiosity that is at the heart of our efforts to extol the skills of the 'pathfinder' as key to being a *Change Maker*.

Case Study – Pathfinder - Research Teams

Cesesma is a community rights-based organisation in Nicaragua. It has been providing examples of how to involve children as researchers since 2007.

In reviewing what had been learnt over the years, Shier et al. (2023) draw on 'sistematizaciøn'. This is a process that at its best leads to a self-facilitated process of assessment. This is 'considered stronger' when adults and children come together.

A framework for this collective process is seen to involve five steps:

(1) Describe the lived experiences.

(2) Describe relevant aspects of contexts or conditions.

(3) Describe what was achieved or outcomes observed at each stage.

(4) Discuss difficulties encountered at each stage.

(5) Review[...]to identify the most important lessons learnt.

(Shier et al., 2023)

As a result, they found the following:

- Skill facilitators and technical support can help to enable children's projects.

- Empowerment is reflected through capacity, opportunity and self-belief (which strongly reflects themes relating to the *Change Maker*).

- Transformations that take place as part of an experience '(1) empowerment of the young researchers (2) transformation of family and social attitudes (3) reflective learning that transforms attitudes, perspectives and practices of adults working with children and (4) transformative social change through action in society'.

- How important it is for young researchers to be actively involved in creating an action plan to support dissemination and to pursue their recommendations.

- The importance of support throughout an organisation to see change implemented.

(Shier et al., 2023)

In addition, this process highlighted the need for children to be seen as 'transformative researchers' reflecting they are more than a 'consultant' brought in to contribute on an issue. Rather, they are embedded in the process, which the team noted 'marked a significant conceptual shift from researcher as outsider to researcher as insider' (Shier et al., 2023). It is this type of change that links to our ambitions here to make being a pathfinder a capability that adds to our sense of identity as a *Change Maker*.[3]

Reflection

Read the following research project that was carried out by Year four learners:

https://wels.open.ac.uk/research/childrens-research-centre/young-voices

How were children involved in the project? What roles did they play? Were adults involved? If so, how did they support the child researchers?

---

(3) Being an Influencer: Strategies to Communicate Are Key to Change

Table 7. Be an Influencer.

Be an Influencer	I have a deep awareness and practical 'know how' to communicate and share their knowledge
	I understand different platforms for amplifying a message
	I recognise skills to express, explain and listen to ideas and opinions

A deep awareness and practical 'know how' to communicate and share their knowledge. This includes an understanding of different platforms for amplifying a message, as well as skills to express, explain and listen to ideas and opinions. Set out in Table 7.

One of the outstanding features of high profile child/youth advocacy, like March for our Lives and Fridays for Future, has been the power of the message.

This reflects both the savvy way in which social media has been used by young people, but also the access they found to present on high profile platforms. However, it is the authentic expression of their voice, their thoughts and their ideas that stands out. In speeches and in the wider messaging that sits around these campaigns, we get a clear sense of the unfettered voice of the child, which is deeply affecting to those that hear it. As we explore the 'influencer', we are compelled by the power of releasing children's voices but also exploring techniques that allow children, if they wish, to 'turn up the volume'. Notably, as well as encouraging children to take a public platform, our interest is in the way children can be 'influencers' within their everyday interactions. The idea of sharing one's own story was a clear theme in the literary examples we considered in Chapter 2. Of course, there is an applied worth to children feeling able to narrate their story, directly impacting those themes of connectedness (*value*, *voice* and *vision*) that we have argued are key to a positive identity as a *Change Maker*.

For many, that unfettered presentation of voice (in its broadest sense), is limited by adult directed practices that reflect the assumptions associated with the *Muted Citizen*. Tokenism is a word that is never far away from participative opportunities. Research on children's role on school councils or local decision-making bodies (see Percy-Smith et al., 2023) regularly shows children are involved more to tick a box rather than to play an active role.

Children have found ways around the barriers that adults create, as seen through school strikes; for example (see Chapter 2), however a continued perception of children as the *Muted Citizen* results in children's voice only being granted status when it is shared at a time and on a subject set by adults. How those contributions are responded to and how they will 'influence' are adult defined. Establishing the *Change Maker* with the capabilities of the influencer, which begins simply by equipping children to recognise the value in their 'authentic voice', demands we escape from children sharing their 'voice' in response to adult frameworks. Opportunities to amplify that authentic voice, once it is found, bring us back to themes of meaningfulness within the context of an individual's personal interactions and encounters. This means recognising the meaning in both that stage that allows mass exposure (for example, a TED talk or speaking at the Lincoln Memorial), but also in the day-to-day interactions that enable a conversation about change with a teacher or allow for ideas to be shared with a local community group or indeed to bring about change within the home. We need to be influenced by children; this requires us not only to ask, but to ensure *their* freedom of opportunity to express themselves. Through extending a belief in their capabilities as an 'influencer', children will be better able to make choices and act outside of the barriers that have for too long restricted children's participation. We recognise this is especially difficult for young people in challenging circumstances.

Influencers – Exploring This in Practice

Amika George, as a teenager, launched a successful campaign to fund period products in schools throughout England. In her book Make it Happen, she sets out a series of activities that focus on how we might have 'influence'. These steps include

- Choose your cause.

- Find your crowd.

- Spread the word.

- Marching matters.

- Prioritise you.

(George, 2021)

It is notable that George's starting point is the need to 'find your power'.

> *I suggest listing all the things you are good at. Every single one. Don't leave anything out. If this feels like a challenge, imagine you're writing about a friend, rather than yourself…List your skills. Are you artistic? Are you good at writing? Are you methodical? Do you like motivating people? List them all down…(George, 2021)*

This is a great way for us to begin our conversations with children. These ideas have relevance to our ambitions to enable the *Change Maker* in the context of those micro-everyday interactions, as well as to recognise the role they can play in a more involved campaign. As we noted above, often the initial hurdle for many children as 'influencers' is to accept that they have something worthy of sharing, and their voice matters (for more practical activities see Frankel & Whalley, 2023 or www.learningallowed.org). As we reflect on voice here, we do so in the broadest sense. We recognise the different presentations of voice as children seek to express themselves through art, music or other creative mediums. Of course, this includes 'voice' for those who are non-verbal, as investment is made in skilled practitioners, strategies and equipment to ensure each individual voice is heard.

Establishing that sense of voice in the context of an 'influencer' needs practice. Such opportunities might come through experiencing a mini campaign (see Part 2). This might lead to inviting children to get involved in

- Writing newsletters.

- Organising a petition.

- Public speaking.

- Running a social media campaign.

(George, 2021)

In order to make the most of such tasks, it is necessary to ensure that there is meaning attached to it – one way of thinking about the meaningfulness of an opportunity, and how it can contribute to extending the capabilities of the 'influencer' is to reflect on whether the activity itself:

- Encourages – builds up the individual (reinforces our focus on 'value').

- Creates – encounters that are relevant.

- Empowers – drives a mutually beneficial agenda.

- Ambitious – recognises the contribution that can be made to a shared goal ('vision').

[This is developed in Chapter 6.]

This can be a useful measure for the facilitator as part of reviewing the nature of opportunities and how they might be maximised, moving beyond tokenism and an adult centric agenda.

Children are demonstrating the power of being an influencer. They are finding ways to ensure that their authentic ideas and opinions are having impact, not just on their peers but on society as a whole. This needs to be encouraged, as we continue to explore the variety of platforms and opportunities that are available; enabling children to confidently, safely and meaningfully share what they have to say. For example, consider social media. Moral panic has intensified around the negative impact social media has had on young people's lives. Risk-based notions about harm (for example, impact on self-esteem, self-image, isolation, mental-health, cyberbullying and exploitation) dominate discussions/discourse about young people's engagement in online spaces (Adorjan & Ricciardelli, 2019; Sticca & Perren, 2013). While there is no doubt, online spaces can be unsafe and can negatively impact the well-being of children and youth; it's important to understand from children's viewpoints how and why they engage in digital spaces and their thoughts on what impacts this can have in their lives. Consider the following case study:

Case Study 1 – Influencer - Child and Youth Engagement in Online Spaces

In this case study, Daniella interviewed young people about their experiences with online engagement and how it impacts their lives. Overwhelmingly, young people had a lot of good things to say about why and how they engage online. For instance, many young people spoke about how it is the one space that isn't controlled by adults and young people can curate their own online identities/ spaces to showcase their thoughts/feelings about certain topics. For example, many young people spoke about their political engagement online, environmental activism, social justice interests and how they could get involved or occupy online spaces in a way that is taken seriously by others (or in a way that doesn't get filtered by adults). Many of the young people spoke about how online engagements can promote and strengthen friendships, romantic relationships, and can act as spaces of belonging and connections; especially for young people who find it difficult to connect with others who are going through something that they are experiencing (such as moving to a new country, finding other young people with similar disabilities, or other youths who identify as LGBTQ2S+). Although some of the young people were acutely aware of the potential harms associated with social media and they outlined that they were sometimes impacted by these factors, it was clear that what they valued was the opportunity to curate their own spaces, messages and ideas, without adult governance and control. They also valued the potential impact their messages/engagements could have (e.g. politically with climate/social justice activism). Most importantly, they were in control of developing/curating/managing their online identities, and this was what the participants really valued.

> **Reflection**
>
> What influence can children have in online spaces? How can children safely exercise agency in online spaces? How can online spaces serve as spaces of influence to enhance children's voices/agency?[4]

Case Study 2 – Influencer - Children as Political Activists

Tokenism must be overcome. In this case study, Gabby Gooch (2023) interviewed members of a steering group set up to provide a youth voice to the Canadian senate about ambitions to lower the voting age to 16. What this investigation showed was the particular value young people felt in being taken seriously and having a part to play in the process. Being an 'influencer' was not necessarily demonstrated by seeing an actual change in policy, but rather believing that their contribution was informing the paradigm shift that has been such a focus of previous chapters. As one of the contributors said,

> *The first step to convincing people to actually participate in government is to show them that their voices are actually being heard and taken into account. If politicians reached out to youth more often and took the time to listen to their opinions or ideas, they might get more of a sense of connection to the government.*

It is notable that even in situations where they knew they were unlikely to see the change they wished for, they were still highly motivated to participate. As Cummings (2020) explains,

> *Having a voice does not mean getting one's way either for adults or for children. Rather, it means participating in the decision-making process both for families and in communities. It means being counted. (p. 31)*

A reason that activating one's capability as an influencer mattered so much to the members of the steering group is that having their voice 'counted', informed their perception of themselves, it added to their sense of identity as a *Change Maker*. It is important not to underestimate how putting into practice capabilities such as being an 'influencer' adds to the way children perceive their identity as a participant. However, it is not good enough to say taking part is where engagement ends; taking part must be seen as merely the starting point in redrawing the paradigm!

Reflection

How can being an influencer impact one's identity? Think about children's participation in relation to the influence they can have. Develop ideas/examples for how children can be meaningfully included in specific processes to have influence.

---

(4) Being a Connecter – Relationships Are Key to Change

Table 8. Be Connectors.

Be Connectors	We can recognise our own feelings and the feeling of others
	We can navigate interactions/encounters effectively

> *Being able to read others and use this as a basis to frame an interaction/encounter is key to being a Change Maker. Pathfinder skills allow knowledge to be gathered; the 'connector' can then assess that knowledge, empathise with it and seek to make connections that result in change. Set out in Table 8.*

Effective community change models are those that build from the bottom up (Leonard, 2013). This acknowledges that imposing a plan that is not representative of the grassroots of that community is likely to be rejected. In the past, children's place in change has been as an observer. As we saw in Chapter 3, 'children rights' emerged from a model of well-meaning adults acting on behalf of the child, advocating on their behalf. This image of advocacy, reflected in many settings, from law to healthcare, sees certain adults, with certain qualifications, acting as interpreters for the change that is needed in children's lives. Our ambition here is to contribute to a way in which children can be at the centre of community change. This requires children taking their place as a key constituent in the process of change where all (adults and children) understand how critical children's involvement is in successful transformation. Rather than an observer, the child here is a 'connector', actively working to join the ambitions of those around them (adults and children) into a shared vision for change.

To enable children to play a part as connectors, it requires that 'shift' we have been talking about to take place. In short, we need to address the 'culture' that influences the spaces that adults and children share. This is reflected in a 'culture of advocacy' (Frankel, 2018), epitomised by a shared commitment to be reflective and to re-examine traditional power hierarchies. In order to 'establish' and 'amplify' the child within everyday social spaces, five steps offer facilitators not just a focus for implementation, but a means to measure and evaluate change through connection:

(1) Re-vitalise your thinking.

(2) Be spatially aware.

(3) Speak the right language.

(4) Create meaningful opportunities.

(5) Lead the change.

(see Chapter 6)

For this process to be effective, however, it requires that both adults and children reposition themselves. In spaces, such as a school, where hierarchies have been relied on as a means of establishing social order, activating this can be a challenge. It is a step that requires an increasing willingness to trust (both adults and children) as a premium is placed on investing in relationships. Notably, the change in relationship is not about removing adult authority (something professionals often fear). Rather, it is about expanding an active willingness to search for and demonstrate a means of engagement that allows the child to feel they are 'known' and 'understood'. It is a mutual respect that drives a culture in which children can be open about their sense of *value*, *voice* and *vision* and through this, review and respond to changes in their levels of connection.

Reference to a 'culture' of advocacy above highlights the need to interrogate institutional norms or practices as part of resetting that relationship. A change in culture and its impact on practice has been reflected in research related frameworks where, for example, workshops are used to enable adults and children to come together to build a practice-based relationships, including shaping the language to enable effective participation. This can be seen on topics such as consent. Rather than a presumption that children understand 'consent', researchers might use workshops to introduce children to what they are being asked to do and to the 'choices' that they have.[5] In the context of the *Change Maker*, what we are suggesting is that this is extended further – through enabling children as connectors, adults and children can come together to shape an understanding of consent that is relevant and applicable to their project – they can shape meaning.

In short, it is important that we do not underestimate the need to focus on, through defined actions and activities, the process of building effective relationships that bring meaning to the way in which all within that space are able to connect with their identity as participants.

Connector – Exploring This in Practice. Connection stems from the individual being able to establish, grow and maintain a positive sense of *value*, *voice* and *vision*. Being a connector is allowing others to do the same.

So much of our research with children reflects a common thread. Children, in their relationships both with other children and with adults, are searching for relationships that reflect mutuality, a level of shared respect, where both feel valued. For the children, a mutual relationship, as mentioned above, is often described in terms of being 'known' or 'understood'. Such relationships are important; they offer a foundation for managing choice and making decisions about right and wrong that define actions or reactions. To equip children to manage such relationships, it is perhaps first important that we raise awareness of the disparity of power that is common in our everyday interactions (children and adults). In our encounters with others, we will find, as part of exercising our agency, a constant process of assessment and review as we consider the nature of the relationship we have. As Sam has written about elsewhere it creates six defining positions that reflect how we see ourselves, but also how we perceive the 'other'.

These categories (set out in Table 9) are as follows:

Table 9. Power Perspectives.

Powerful self	Powerful other
Powerless self	Powerless other
Mutual self	Mutual other

By reflecting on these categories with children, we can start to enhance both 'theirs' and 'our' capabilities to assess relationships, from which we can collaborate effectively in shaping change.

In understanding power and finding ways to effectively respond, a skill such as listening can be invaluable. However, as Nancy Kline (2020) suggests, listening is not only important as part of building relationships but in extending the way the individual feels empowered to think independently. Our ambitions for a common good demand that both adults and children are willing to break free from the chains that have restricted effective participation in the past. It means that both sides need the space to be more independent in their thinking of the other, but also of themselves. Kline makes a powerful case for the value in creating that space within relationships to listen. With obvious crossovers to the influencer above, these skills seem highly relevant in creating that culture that allows one another to thrive. Here the focus on listening gives a sense of the practical and accessible way in which we might all be involved in building better relationships that extend the freedoms and generate connections for meaningful participation.

What is significant about this emphasis on the 'connector' in the context of everyday tasks like listening is that it extends how and where we might look for opportunities for participation. Notably, as we have been saying throughout, a focus on the everyday nature of participation has an important transformative power (O'Sullivan et al., 2023; Percy-Smith, 2018). This requires an awareness of what everyday participation is:

> *[It is] the right to participate in intergenerational dialogic encounters within multiple social processes embedded in everyday contexts and interactions, and encompassing both decision making and non decision making moments.*
>
> *(O'Sullivan, 2021, p. 63 - cited in O'Sullivan et al., 2023, p. 38)*

This broad definition defines the multiple opportunities that then exist to support children's engagement in community interactions. Notably O'Sullivan et al. (2023) talk of how such participation is reflected in safe, respectful relationships that are reciprocal and where the individual feels listened to. By being able to draw attention to 'participation' in this everyday understanding, O'Sullivan et al. suggest how it adds to children's ability and confidence to be part of decision-making moments, trusting the value of their involvement within a partnership that holds meaning. Without the paradigm shift, we are arguing for it 'impedes their [children's] lived participation as it does not render children free to spontaneously, without risk, enter intergenerational dialogic process' (O'Sullivan et al., 2023, p. 39).

To move beyond a sense of fear that might constrain engagement, this work suggests steps such as

- Children taking leadership roles.

- Self and peer assessment.

- Co-construction of knowledge.

- 'Teachers' (other adults) presenting as non-expert.

- Children take initiative. (p. 41)

All of which demand that children are aware of their capabilities as connectors, seeking to build positive relationships that allow the community as a whole to grow.

Case Study - Connector - Children and Adults - A Partnership

In a valuable insight into a movement of working children in Peru, Jessica Taft (2019) illustrates the importance of relationships in projects focused on social change.

A foundation for this is an awareness of the active and meaningful role that children can play in society. Represented by the term 'protagonisimo' (see Cussianovich, 2001), we are presented with an emerging image of the child that challenges traditional Spanish colonial discourses in which 'to be childlike [...]was to be both unruly and sinful and therefore, in need of religious education and moral guidance' (2019, p. 47). With similarities to our discussion in Chapter 2, the protagonismo rejects a passive role. Rather, it is defined by an active sense of 'collective agency in political and social life' (2019, p. 63). From this starting point, Taft (2019) highlights how an acceptance of this 'image' of the child provides a foundation for relationships with adults that pave the way for 'change'.

Establishing productive relationships means addressing power. Taft (2019) reflects on this in relation to

- Equality of dignity.

- Equality of capacity.

- Equality of insight.

Whether these are used in the context of inter or intra generational relationships, they provide a valuable means for reflecting on relationships and building and enabling meaningful connections.

Equality of dignity: Centred around the equal worth of everyone – adult or child; this call for a shared humanity reflects best those wider international efforts around children's rights. It, therefore, has a level of credence that leads to Taft (2019) suggesting it is the most easily implemented. Practically, naming practices offer a means to address power, for example inviting everyone to be referred to by their first name.

Equality of capacity: The reality expressed here is that engaging in social movements takes time and involves experience. Recognising what can be shared between individuals on that basis allows group members to look beyond age.

Equality of insight: It is through an acceptance of the ongoing learning journeys that we are all on that Taft (2019) suggests we can maximise social and political contributions. It demands an awareness that both children and adults have something to offer, bringing unique and individualised perspectives to any given issue. It is only by embracing the need to extend our own understanding through inviting meaningful collaborations that change is made possible.

This short extract goes a small way to introduce the practical ways in which adults and children are creating relationships that open up opportunities for change. Having an explicit focus on 'being a connector' adds to the scope and depth of possible partnerships.

CONCLUSION

How good are we at reflecting on our own capabilities? The tests we take are often linked to academic subjects and certain intellectual ways of thinking, but how often do we stop and question our capabilities to navigate the social world we are part of? This chapter has highlighted the importance of asking those questions. If we are to extend the freedoms we have, adding to the richness of our lives and our sense of life satisfaction, then investing in our capabilities is critical. Through the four capabilities discussed above, we offer a basis to begin a process of reflection that allows for a detailed enquiry into our capabilities. As we stated at the start of the chapter, this is not about grading who is a better 'learner/pathfinder/influencer/connector' than others, but more about opening a means through which each can explore our own personal goals and set targets to achieve our own personal bests. The attributes reviewed here are a means for shaping and adding to our journeys of personal discovery. What we have suggested is that having strengthened your sense of connection through considering one's *value, voice* and *vision* as a learner (in the broadest sense); we are then set to advance our capabilities to bring about change!

It is our desire to now put this all into practice.

NOTES

1.   Sen divides this between 'opportunity aspect', a focus on the actual outcomes and 'process' aspect, with a focus on all possible outcomes.
2.   https://www.thersa.org/blog/2016/07/education-the-enlightenment-and-the-21st-century
3.   Safeguarding and the role of strong relationships with parents, family and members of the local community and the role of 'adolescents' as enablers also emerge as an important aspect of enabling effective research (see Shier et al., 2023 for more).
4.   For more see Percy-Smith et al. (2023) and Vickery (2017).
5.   For an interesting discussion on consent, see Mountford and Vento (2023).

PART 2

5

INTRODUCING CHANGE MAKER CLUBS

It's time to get practical.

In this second part of the book, we set out a series of workshops designed to support you in setting up a 'Change Maker' club or group.

The 'club' was an idea that we thought of a few years ago whilst working with some university students and children. Bringing together motivated students with passionate and engaged groups of children, created an energy and dynamic that we wanted to replicate.

Below, we set out a series of workshops that will allow you to begin to build your own club, bringing together facilitators and children as part of expanding this vision for the 'Change Maker'. The formation of your team of facilitators will differ and will be shaped by those with a passion to get involved from your community. In a university context, we recognise the potential of young adults but know that many others could be part of your team.

In relation to children, the content below is set out for those aged around 8–12 years old. In keeping with many of the arguments in Part 1, we do not wish to be prescriptive as we both have worked with groups, older and younger, using similar activities. However, children aged 8–12 years old often find themselves underrepresented, and it is for that reason that we seek to focus on this age range (although feel free to adapt as needed)!

We are very aware that any club or group that you create will look different from those in other communities, and we welcome that. Our hope is that you will feel confident to just give it a go. This may mean as follows:

- Running a full-scale club or group on an ongoing basis.

- Running a taster session to pilot and test out some ideas.

- Delivering some workshops linked to the capabilities in local schools/
community spaces.

For those who are reading this and are thinking, I have no plans of setting up a group/club, don't worry. The content in the following chapters can be used to support learning, with a range of tasks and methods to encourage practical experiences to advance capabilities that enhance children's participation.

The following chapters are set out in Table 10 as follows:

Table 10. Part 2 Overview.

Chapter	Theme/Focus	Workshop
6	Facilitating Change Making	1.1 Revitalise your thinking
		1.2 Be spatially aware
		1.3 Speak the right language
		1.4 Create meaningful opportunities
		1.5 Lead the change
7	Being a Pathfinder	2.1 Have an idea
		2.2 Talk, listen and plan
		2.3 Give it a go
		2.4 Keep on learning
		2.5 A project
8	Being an Influencer	3.1 Your voice matters
		3.2 Using your voice
		3.3 Expressing your ideas
9	Being a Connector	4.1 Relationship building
		4.2 Understanding others
		4.3 Planning your project

Chapters 7–9 reflect those capabilities of the *Change Maker* we raise in Chapter 4. In Chapter 4, we do also discuss a fourth capability – 'being a learner, for more on developing this and exploring '*value, voice* and *vision*', see Learning Allowed (Frankel & Whalley, 2023).

This content will be supported on www.learningallowed.org

A PRACTICAL GUIDE TO DELIVERING THE WORKSHOPS

Content

Each chapter is focused on a different topic as outlined in the table above. The table shows that each topic is divided into themes that are reflected in a series of 'workshops':

We have set out an order to support delivery; however, there is flexibility for groups to run their own programme.

Each workshop is divided into a series of activities.

Layout

Each chapter is set out in the same way.

Each workshop starts with providing the following information for facilitators:

- 'Aim': this will provide the facilitator with information about the theme.

- 'Objectives': the defined goals of that workshop.

- 'Resources/delivery': any resources or relevant delivery information that is required.

- [For Chapter 6] 'Part 1 reference points': to help you link back to what you will have read from the first part of the book.

Each activity then breaks down into a 'script' to enable delivery, using the following format:

- 'Explain': text that can be paraphrased to your participants explaining the activity.

- 'Invite': sets out the tasks the participants can undertake.

- 'Reflect': encourages the group to review what has been learnt and how it may be applied.

- 'Note': any guidance or ideas that we think might be useful.

Delivery

Each workshop will take around 40–60 mins to deliver although you can adapt as needed.

Designing a programme for delivery: the content below is there for you to develop and adapt into a programme that will work for you. Although do let us know how you get on!

Activities – group size: we refer throughout the activities to learning in 'small groups'. Next to these we have suggested a group size, but this is just for guidance and of course you can adapt as necessary. A note of caution: more than six children in a group often limits the space for each individual to contribute fully so we recommend capping the groups at six.

Finding a Group and Running a Club

You need two groups to deliver a project

(1) Facilitators – those that can enable the activities of the club.

(2) Members – those who can take part.

We have made suggestions above about who these might be (for e.g. undergraduate students as facilitators, young children as participants).

It will be up to you to ensure that you comply with all relevant policies, legislation, ethical standards and guidance to deliver your project, including safeguarding.

For support in setting up a club, contact us – www.learningallowed.org

Below we offer a starting point and a way forward to get you started!

6

FACILITATING CHANGE MAKING – IN PRACTICE

FACILITATOR INTRODUCTION

The point of this chapter and the related workshop is to build confidence as a team in establishing a positive 'culture' where the *Change Maker* can flourish.

How we think about children and how children think about themselves matters.

It shapes practices and defines experiences. A culture of advocacy (Frankel, 2018) introduced in Chapter 4 suggests five steps that help us to question, review, amend and maintain an enabling environment that encourages *all* to explore what it means to be a *Change Maker*.

We draw on these five steps here to offer a practical guide to setting up that culture and maintaining it.[1]

(1) Revitalise your thinking – keep questioning assumptions.

(2) Be spatially aware – does your rhetoric match reality.

(3) Speak the right language.

(4) Create meaningful opportunities.

(5) Lead the change.

OVERVIEW PLAN

Set out in Table **11**.

Table 11. Overview Chapter 6.

Theme/Focus	Workshop	Activities
Facilitating change making	1.1 Revitalise your thinking	1.1.1: Assumptions
		1.1.2: Image of the child
		1.1.3: Reflection
		1.1.4: Shifting attitudes
	1.2 Be spatially aware	1.2.1: A culture for change
		1.2.2: Understanding participation
		1.2.3: Rhetoric v reality
		1.2.4: Sharing a vision
	1.3 Speak the right language	1.3.1: Talking about participation
		1.3.2: What is a *Change Maker?*
		1.3.3: Reflection
	1.4 Create meaningful opportunities	1.4.1: Meaningful opportunities
		1.4.2: Reviewing opportunities
	1.5 Lead the change	1.5.1: Skills audit
		1.5.2: Being the change
		1.5.3: Reflection

1.1 Revitalise Your Thinking – Question Assumptions

Workshop Guidance

Aim: The activities are focused on challenging assumptions and inviting the group to question how they view children and how this might impact on the way they act (the practices they employ). Of course, these actions ultimately shape children's experiences.

Objectives:

- Be aware of how assumptions impact thinking on children.

- Be aware of our own assumptions.

- Be aware of how a shift in assumptions creates possibilities for the 'Change Maker'.

Resources/Delivery:
Paper/cardstock/pens/markers.

Activity 1.1.2: Prior to the workshop, make a pack of cards (with paper or cardstock) that include words on them for each group. The words should reflect characteristics of the *Muted Citizen* and the *Change Maker* from Chapter 2.

For example,
Muted Citizen: Disruptive, Blank Slate, Impressionable, Passive, Subject.
Change Maker: Active, Connected, Mearing Maker, Being and Becoming.

Part 1 reference points: Chapter 2

Activity 1.1.1 – Assumptions
Explainer: The aim is to think about assumptions and how this impacts children.

Invite: the participants to get into small groups (3 or 4) and ask them to reflect on the following questions:

(1) Think of some assumptions that you hold about children.

(2) Are these assumptions limiting – if so, why?

(3) Watch the following video from Radi-Aid – a former awareness raising campaign project: https://www.youtube.com/watch?v=xbqA6o8_WC0

(4) What are your thoughts about the video?

Reflect: What assumptions can you recognise from your own experiences that limit or restrict children's participation?

Activity 1.1.2 – The Image of Child
Explain: Assumptions surround the way we think about children, and as a result, the way children think about themselves (see Chapter 2).

Invite: the groups, on one piece of paper, to draw a visual interpretation of the 'Muted Citizen' and on another, to draw an interpretation of the 'Change Maker' (do not label them). Make them sit at opposite ends of the table.

[**Note:** ensure that each group has their own set of the words that you prepared before the session, see the guidance above.]
Then ask the following questions:

(Continued)

First,

- Which words characterise the *Muted Citizen*?

- Why have you chosen those words?

- What day to day practices ensure some children are *Muted Citizens*?

Second,

- Which words characterise the *Change Maker*?

- Why have you chosen those words?

- What day to day practices enable some children to be *Change Makers*?

Reflect: What can we learn from this activity that might help with preparing or running a *Change Makers* Club? (For example: what 'image' do you have of the child and why does that matter?)

Activity 1.1.3 – Reflection

Invite: your participants to deepen their thinking by using some of the sections marked 'reflection' in Chapter 2.

Pick those reflections that you think will support your group best.

Activity 1.1.4 – Shifting Attitudes

Explain: Assumptions shape adult thinking, but they also shape the way children think about themselves. In the context of your 'club', this process should encourage children to question assumptions about their role as participants but also their assumptions about adults.

Invite: small groups (4 or 5) to respond to the following questions by picking keywords/short phrases.

Capture responses using large sheets of paper and coloured pens. Use a separate sheet for each question (and each group).

[**Note:** the aim is to run this activity with members of your 'club' – your facilitator team and your child 'Change Makers'.]

Ask the adults [your team of facilitators]:

- How do you see children?

- How do you see adults (yourself)?

- What does it mean to be a *Change Maker*?

Ask the children [your participants]:

- How do you see children (yourself)?

- How do you see adults?

- What does it mean to be a *Change Maker?*

Reflect: Review the adult and child answers alongside each other. Do they align? Use this to drive a conversation about assumptions!

Note: It is always interesting to recognise the similarities and differences between the ways in which children and adults see each other – what does this tell us about children and childhood?

1.2 Be Spatially Aware – Rhetoric and Reality

Workshop Guidance

Aim: Having explored our assumptions, we can now think about the spaces that we share with children. To what extent are those spaces informed by adult assumptions or are they spaces where adults and children hold a shared vision and ambition?

Part of the challenge is that adults are really good at saying certain things (rhetoric) – 'we welcome children's voices', but this is not always followed in practice (reality). Our aim is to see if we can get rhetoric and reality to align in a positive way.

Objectives:

- To recognise what shapes a culture for participation.

- Be aware of the rhetoric you use – how you might align this to reality in a positive way.

Resources/Delivery:

Paper/pens/markers.

Copies of the participation continuum from Chapter 1.

(Continued)

Part 1 reference points: Chapters 1 and 2.

Activity 1.2.1 – A Culture for Change

Invite: the group to respond to this question:

- What are the key ingredients of a 'space' or environment that enables the *Change Maker?*

Think about your club – what will be important to get right in establishing a culture to encourage participation?

Reflect: A key ingredient must be opportunities for conversations. How did your answers reflect this?

Activity 1.2.2 – Understanding Participation

Explain: It is important for any team to be aware that the way we (adults) come to speak about participation can be very different from the reality of children's experiences.

Invite: the group to look at the participation continuum (see Chapter 1). Ask:

- How might the continuum be used as a feedback tool with children? (see note)

- What would you need to do to put it into practice?

- How would you ensure that children's responses are followed up?

Note: having a visual of the continuum and inviting a child to identify where they sit on this line provides a chance to assess whether they feel closer to the *Change Maker* or *Muted Citizen.* This can encourage conversations about

- Why do they feel like this?

- What is working well or not so well?

Activity 1.2.3 - Rhetoric v Reality

Explain: Rhetoric (the way we talk about children and our project) and reality (children's experiences) can easily find themselves out of alignment. As a group, it is important to remain vigilant that we keep rhetoric and reality aligned.

Invite: the group to look at any written material you have for your club (or if you don't have any material for your club – think about how you would want to present your *Change Maker* project). Look at or think about the wording/images on/in any:

- Posters.
- Flyers.
- Activity Packs.
- Websites.
- Social Media.

Reflect:

- Are you presenting an image of children as *Change Makers* or *Muted Citizens?*
- Are you sharing a motivation driven by the *Change Maker* or *Muted Citizen?*

Note: Increasingly invite children to be part of this reflection with you and continue to reflect on this as you develop your project and materials.

Activity 1.2.4 – Sharing a Vision

Explain: It is important to find ways in which children feel meaningfully involved in communicating the ambitions of the club.

Invite: set targets for some new ways of sharing the voices of children – an audio message, cartoons or wherever your imagination leads. Reflect on these new ways of sharing children's voices to ensure they are focused on the *Change Maker* and not the *Muted Citizen.*

1.3 Speak the Right Language

Workshop Guidance

Aim: To establish a shared language that supports the change maker in your community. Having a language that allows the whole team (facilitators and members) to come together is an important component of furthering that culture discussed in the last workshop.

Objective:

- To identify keywords that reflect the values of your project.

(Continued)

- To have a definition of these words.

- To know how these are put into practice.

Resources/Delivery:

You will need pens and large sheets of paper, being able to hang ideas around the room will help.

Part 1 reference points: Chapters 3 and 4.

Activity 1.3.1 – Talking About Participation

Explain: How we talk about 'participation' can be contentious. It can differ. Chapter 3 highlights this as it explores language around rights and models of participation. A response to this is to work collectively to establish a shared language that has meaning when you are talking about the *Change Maker* and participation.

Invite: small groups to answer this question:

- What is participation? Write down your responses.

Reflect:

- Did you find similarities with your definition? What key characteristics of participation were discussed?

- How might differing understandings of participation be a challenge for your club/any group working with children?

Activity 1.3.2 – What Is a Change Maker?

Invite: the group to answer this question:

- What is a *Change Maker*?

Reflect:

How did your definition match ours:

> *'Change Maker' is a sense of identity.*
>
> *It is a way to think about ourselves as free to access and maximise opportunities that are meaningful in shaping how we view our participation; contributing to positive change(s) in our communities (micro or macro).*

Explain: A clear definition of the *Change Maker* will help you to create opportunities to develop capabilities.

Invite: have a look at Table 12 below – how might you adopt it? What changes might you need to make to work for your 'club'?

Reflect: How can children be involved in this process? How will you make sure you keep updating it over time?

Activity 1.3.3 – Reflection

Invite: the group to respond to some of the sections marked 'reflections' in Chapter 10. Think about the changing nature of participation and how having a practical and accessible definition of the 'Change Maker' is so important.

Table 12. Change Maker Capabilities (Linked to Activity 1.3.2).

	Capabilities	Attributes
Change Maker	Be a Learner	I can make sense, manage and take control of a learning journey
		I can connect with a sense of value, voice and vision
	Be a Pathfinder	I am a knowledge creator
		I know how to design research
		I am confident in asking questions and capturing and making sense of the answers
	Be an Influencer	I have a deep awareness and practical 'know how' to communicate and share their knowledge
		I understand different platforms for amplifying a message
		I recognise skills to express, explain and listen to ideas and opinions
	Be Connectors	We can recognise our own feelings and the feeling of others
		We can navigate interactions/encounters effectively

1.4 Create Meaningful Opportunities

Workshop Guidance

Aim: It is important to remain reflexive as we engage and develop tasks and activities with children. How and in what ways are these activities meaningful and how do they contribute to being a *Change Maker*? Such questions invite us to think carefully about the nature of the activities we then create. The opportunities here reflect an ambition to:

(Continued)

- Encourage each individual.

- Create relevant experiences.

- Empower the *Change Maker*.

- Be ambitious in scope.

Objectives:

- To reflect on what shapes a meaningful opportunity.

- To identify ways of reviewing meaningfulness and enhancing what you offer.

Resources/Delivery:
Pens and paper.
Printouts of the tables referred to.
Part 1 reference points: Chapter 4

Activity 1.4.1 – Meaningful Opportunities
Explain: How we participate is reflected in the meaning we attach to an encounter. Below are four measures that you can use to explore meaningfulness.
Invite the group to review/discuss the following questions:
Encourage:

- Do participants recognise their *value, voice* and *vision*?

- Do participants feel they are able to develop their capabilities as *Change Makers?*

Create:

- Are participants actively involved in defining the activities and programs?

- Are children partners in creating content that is relevant and accessible?

Empower:

- Are participants able to shape and define the culture of your change making clubs?

- Are children involved in review and evaluation?

Be Ambitious:

- In what ways is each individual member of the club able to recognise and celebrate their journey as a *Change Maker?*

Reflect:

- What are your thoughts?

- How would you develop this for use with your club?

Activity 1.4.2 – Reviewing Opportunities

Invite: the group to reflect on Table 1.4.2 (Table 13) and provide their input into it.

Reflect:

- What would you prioritise as a starting point?

- How often do you think you should plan a review of your club and the work you have been doing? Set dates and commit.

- How can children be increasingly involved in this review process?

Table 13. Meaningful Opportunities (Links to Activity 1.4.2).

What is the setting?			
Who are going to be involved in this opportunity?			
What characteristics/ attributes would you like children to experience as part of this opportunity?			
What is this opportunity?			
This opportunity/platform...	**How is this visible?**	**How might this be added to?**	**Your action steps**
Encourages the individual			
Creates relevant experiences			
Empowers children as change makers			
Is *Ambitious* in scope and intended outcomes			

Source: Frankel (2018).

1.5 Lead the Change

Workshop Guidance
Aim: To recognise and embrace the impact that you can have as a 'Change Maker' in your own right, championing others to explore their identity as *Change Makers.*

Objectives:

- To understand your capabilities and your role

- To recognise the way in which you can enable others in driving a paradigm shift

Resources/Delivery:
   Paper/pens/markers.

Part 1 reference points: Chapter 1

Activity 1.5.1 – Skill Audit
Explain: To take on a paradigm shift (a new way of seeing the world that changes olds ideas), it is important to be aware of skills/capabilities you have as a group.

Invite:

- Individually – identify what skills you have and what skills you would like to develop (write these down).

- In small groups – combine your answers – what matches and what differs from one another (write these down)

- Whole team – combine your answers – what matches and what differs from everyone (write these down)

Reflect:
In the context of delivering your club and adding to a 'paradigm shift' review:

- What skills do you think are important to encourage children as 'Change Makers'?

- How can you continue to develop and encourage those skills?

- What areas (as a team) do you think you need to develop?

- What can you do to enable this (for e.g. training, bringing in new team members)?

Activity 1.5.2 – Being the Change

Explain: this quote from Chapter 1 sets out how to create a paradigm shift:

> *In a nutshell, you keep pointing at the anomalies and failures in the old paradigm, you keep coming yourself, loudly and with assurance from the new one, and you insert people with the new paradigm in places of public visibility and power. You don't waste time with reactionaries; rather you work with active change agents and with the vast middle ground of people who are open minded.*
>
> *(Alexander & Conrad, 2022, p. 165)*

Invite: as you consider this quote ask these questions:

- Are you clear about the paradigm you are trying to see shift? (The move from the *Muted Citizen* to the *Change Maker*)?

- What actions could you take to promote this shift?

Reflect: How will you ensure you review, evaluate, capture and share any paradigm shift resulting from your project? Write down these ideas.

Activity 1.5.3 – Reflection

Invite: the group to respond to some of the sections marked as 'reflections' in Chapter 4.

How might this add to the way you think about your capabilities and those of others.

NOTE

1. For more see Frankel (2018, 2023a, 2023b).

7

BEING A PATHFINDER – IN PRACTICE

Table 6. Be a Pathfinder.

Be a Pathfinder	I am a knowledge creator
	I know how to design research
	I am confident in asking questions and capturing and making sense of the answers

Table 6: Being a pathfinder is inspired by projects that have involved children as researchers. Our viewpoint is that children can participate in research projects, but they can also be leaders in developing, designing and also facilitating research. In order for this to happen, children cannot be treated or viewed as *Muted Citizens*; rather, they need to be able to identify as *Change Makers* and feel as if they can access research opportunities that are meaningful in shaping how they view their participation in them. This can lead to positive changes in their communities, but this requires a shift in how adults think about children's capabilities to engage in research, re-consider what counts as research and the various opportunities that can enable children's leadership/participation in research. To help do this, below we share a child-centred framework for enhancing children's pathfinder capabilities.

In Chapter 4, we shared the following reflective questions:

- Who conceives the project?

- Who selects the methods?

- Who does the work of finding out what needs to be found out?

- Who does the analysis?

- Who interprets the work to the outside world?

(Thomas, 2017, p. 162)

The model below seeks to position 'children' as the answer to these questions.

The format we use to explore what it means to be a pathfinder – follow a model for managing and navigating a task set out in Learning Allowed (Frankel & Whalley, 2023).

AN OVERVIEW PLAN: SET OUT IN TABLE 14

Table 14. Overview Chapter 7

Theme/Focus	Workshop	Activities
Being a Pathfinder	2.1 Have an idea	2.1.1: Pathfinder skills
		2.1.2: Being curious
		2.1.3: Questions
	2.2 Talk, listen and plan	2.2.1: Open & closed questions
		2.2.2: Who to question
		2.2.3: How to question
		2.2.4: Practice...
		2.2.5: How to keep people safe
	2.3 Give it a go	2.3.1: Try it out
	2.4 Keep on learning	2.4.1: What have we discovered?
		2.4.2: Have you got an answer?
		2.4.3: Share what you have discovered
		2.4.4: Reflect and review
	2.5 A project	2.5.1: Researching children's rights
	Research ethics – guidance for facilitators	

Note: This format can be used first to train a team to understand what it means to be a 'pathfinder' and second to run ongoing research projects.

2.1 Have an Idea

Workshop Guidance
Aim: Here we explore what it means to be a pathfinder – a social reporter. In practice, being a pathfinder involves a whole range of skills such as

- Question design.

- Picking who to ask and how.

- Collecting responses.

- Making sense of your findings.

- Sharing what you have to discover.

This exercise invites your team to think a little more about these skills as they prepare to launch a pathfinder project.

Objective:

- Understanding your skills.

- Recognising the skills of others.

- Being aware of the skills of a pathfinder – social reporter.

Resources/Delivery:
Paper/pens/markers

Split the children into groups (ideally with about four people in each). You might wish to write the 'explanation' (the information above) on a flip chart or in a document so the groups can refer to it.

Activity 2.1.1 – Pathfinder Skills
Explain: Being a pathfinder is a bit like being a detective, as you investigate and explore what's going on in the lives of people around you. A pathfinder

- Spots gaps in our knowledge – something we don't know.

- Uses questions to discover more.

- Captures answers and makes sense of them.

- Shares their findings to start conversations that lead to change.

Invite: the participants to

- Draw a picture of themselves.

(Continued)

- Inside the picture of themselves, write any skills they have as a pathfinder.

- Outside themselves, write any skills they wish to develop.

Reflect: As a team, review the skills you have and the skills you might need to develop.

Note: being a pathfinder involves

- Being imaginative – having a good idea.

- Being a great communicator – knowing how to ask questions and to whom.

- Being analytical – making sense of the answers you receive.

- Being a designer/writer/presenter – finding ways to share your ideas with others so they have an impact

It involves a whole range of skills – connect this to the individuals in the group and help group members recognise their skills and identify skills they wish to strengthen.

Activity 2.1.2 – Being Curious
Note:
This task has two parts:

Part A: Being curious – 2.1.2

Part B: Questions' – 2.1.3

Split the room into different 'zones'. The point of each zone is to encourage the children to come up with questions, relating to different issues in a variety of settings. These zones could focus on

- school,

- playground,

- home,

- online spaces,

- out of school clubs,

- green spaces and

- your favourite places.

You can include some prompts in each zone. Some information about the different spaces, for example

- Online Spaces: A news story about children online.

- Community Playground: A photo of a traditional playground alongside one designed by children.

- Green Spaces: A web link to children talking about how they use outdoor spaces

Think of some prompts for each space to help encourage the children to come up with questions – something they would like to know about *each* space.

Split the team into pairs and give each a means to record their ideas (paper/pen or tablet).

Explain: Remind the group that being a pathfinder is all about being curious; any investigation must start with an idea. This task has two parts.

A: Being curious

B: Coming up with questions

Invite: each pair to spend time in each 'zone' and ask them to come up with 'an idea' – something they are curious about. Write down their ideas – what would they like to investigate/be curious about?

Reflect: What 'ideas' did groups come up with? How did ideas compare? What were the common 'ideas' people had?

Activity 2.1.3 – Questions
Explain: 'An idea' that a pathfinder is searching for to build a project around is

- A question no one has the answer to yet.

- A question you can actually investigate.

Invite: the team as a whole to think about:

- What is a question no one has the answer to yet:

(Continued)

[Think about whether the information can be found in books, online and by asking people]

- What is a question you can actually investigate:

[Have you got the resources to find some answers – can you access the people you might need to speak to?]

Reflect: Using the responses from Part 2.1.2 – invite the team to think about which of these ideas would be good for a pathfinder team to investigate and why. Write down your ideas and justifications.

2.2 Talk, Listen and Plan

Workshop Guidance
Aim: We are encouraging you here to explore what a project might look like in practice.

Continue to work with 'an idea' from the previous activity – the questions the children came up with. Use these as examples to support the tasks below.

In this workshop and the activities to follow, we will think through

- Open and closed questions – 2.2.1

- Who to question – 2.2.2

- How to question them – 2.2.3

- How to keep participants 'safe' – 2.2.4

Objectives:

- What are open and closed questions.

- What methods/ways we can ask questions.

- To think about the fairness and safety of anyone involved in research.

Resources/Delivery:
Paper/pens/markers

Use the questions you generated from activity 2.1.3. Use these as a foundation to explore 'open and closed questions' and the different 'methods' in the activities below.

Note: There is a lot in this session. Don't be afraid to take your time in developing your understanding. The time you need will depend on the experience you already have as researchers.

Activity 2.2.1 – Open and Closed Questions

Part A

Explain: There are different types of questions.

- A closed question which has a fixed answer – 'yes', 'no', 'don't know'

- An open question which has a flexible answer, as someone responds to a question that begins with 'who', 'how', 'why', 'what', 'when', 'where' and 'what do you know about research'?

Invite: the groups to think about some open and closed questions. Here are some examples:

- Are you able to balance on one leg?

- What's your favourite food?

- How much time do you spend online?

- Are you funny?

Extend the activity[...]

Set a focus – a research question and create a series of questions and ask the children to think about:

- If it is an open or closed question.

- Whether it is a relevant question – a question no one has the answers to yet/a question you can investigate.

For example:
Focus: to find out how people like to relax after school:

- Where do you like to go on holiday?

- Do you take part in any clubs after school?

(*Continued*)

- Is there wildlife near where you live?

- What do you enjoy doing when you get home after school?

Reflect:

- Could you spot the open or closed questions?

- How might you use them?

- What makes a question relevant or not?

Part B

Explain: Next, we need to come up with

- One big 'open' question that we can build the project around.

- Some mini questions (3 or 4) 'open' questions to investigate parts of our big question.

For example (taken from a research team project):

Big question: To investigate how children at 'our' school use technology in their spare time.

Mini questions – for this team, they split into a focus on video games & social networking.

Video Games:

- What types of games do children play?

- Why do children play video games?

- When do children play video games?

Social Networking:

- Why do children use social networking?

- What safety issues do they think about?

- Has anyone been bullied online, what did they do?

Invite:

As a team: pick one of the ideas from your previous activity – which would you like to investigate? Agree on a 'big question'.

In small groups: come up with some mini questions that will help you to explore this 'big question'.

Reflect: Keep asking yourselves:

- Is this a question no one has the answer to yet

- Is this a question you can actually investigate

Activity 2.2.2 – *Who to Question*

Invite: each group to list all the people they would need to speak to in order to find an answer.

Example – our mini question is 'what new equipment is needed on the playground'?

You may wish to speak to: children who use the playground or some adults who know the playground.

Reflect: explore the list of people you have chosen to speak to.

Activity 2.2.3 – *How to Question*

Explain: You have identified people you want to speak to; next, you need to think about how you speak to them. There are lots of ways to ask a question; you need to pick the right one.

Alternative Option: reflect on Fig. 12 below– there are lots of different ways to ask questions.

Invite: each group to focus on their mini question(s)[...]

(1) Take your list of people above.

(2) Think which method would help you discover an answer – link a method to each group

- A questionnaire – ask 10 closed questions to lots of people – total 20 to 100 people.

- A focus group – ask 5 open questions to 3 groups of 5 people – total 10–15 people.

- An interview – ask 5 open questions to 1 or 2 people – aim for 4–6 interviews
  You should now have a list of people which are linked to a method.

(3) Choose how many you will speak to.

(4) When you will speak to them.

(5) Where you will speak to them.

(Continued)

Use Table 15 below to develop your ideas and see what you come up with then come back to reflect.

Reflect: Discuss your ideas with the rest of the group. Are you feeling confident about how you might use different methods?

Note: If your team has no experience of research, you will want to create a series of additional activities to introduce these different methods to them. More resources will be available at www.learningallowed.org

Activity 2.2.4 – Practice[. . .]

You may find it helpful to practise the use of different methods.
Create some scenarios that give the children the chance to:

- Design a questionnaire.

- Design a focus group and try running it.

- Do mock interviews with one another.

You may want to extend this activity to include other methods too. It is really valuable to give children the chance to practise using the methods they want to include in their project. Then you can get them to reflect on what works and what doesn't and how they can use these observations to inform the way they carry out their methods.

Activity 2.2.5 – How to Keep People Safe

Note: Ethics is complicated. There is much that could be shared. To support facilitators, we have provided some additional guidance on ethics in the Appendices. You may want to explore this within your leadership team.

Explain: It is really important to make sure that you approach your research in a fair way and look after anyone who takes part.

Invite: Groups to discuss these questions:

- What does it mean to treat someone fairly in research?

- What steps could you take to make sure people feel looked after?

Reflect:
Have a look at the guidance sheet below - Table 16. How did this reflect your conversation? How can you make sure you put this into practice?

Methods Guidance - Action 12 - Resources Sheet 5

Method	Description	Advantages	Disadvantages
Interviews	Ask another person questions. *Your role* to decide what type of interview and what questions to ask.	- Great to explore people's feelings - Investigate ideas in detail - Can ask lots of open questions	- Leading questions or closed questions might limit the information you get. - You will need to make a record of your interview this can take time. - You need to practice your interviewing techniques.
	A helpful note: There are 3 types of interview: Structured – you have a clear plan, Semi-structured – you have a bit of a plan, Unstructured – no plan		
Focus Groups	Ask a group of about 5 people to explore the issues. *Your role* to guide the conversation, for this you will need to prepare some questions.	- It can be a great way to include people. - You can get different people's opinions.	- You will need to practice your focus group skills. - The group can lose direction. - Your role is just to support the conversation not to direct it.
Observation	Watch what is going on and make notes. *Your role* to think about what you want to be looking out for. Then to watch but not interfere.	- You can look at action in real life.	- A clear plan is essential. - If people know they are being watched they might behave in a different way to normal. - It is important to watch as an outsider, to look for things you might not normally see.
Questionnaire	Write down some questions and then let people answer them. *Your role* to decide what type of questionnaire and what questions to ask.	- It can allow you to ask lots of people. - It gives you data you can turn into numbers that you can use to help you present your findings.	- You can't go into too much detail. - The design of the questionnaire is important. - You will need to think very carefully about the type of questions that you ask.
	A helpful note: A questionnaire might allow you to support your research through putting your findings into numbers - 10 out of 100 think this – it can be a useful means for sharing your findings.		
Creative/ Action based methods	Photographs Videos Drawing Maps Drama	A range of ideas that are really good for getting people involved and investigating the issues in a slightly different way. If you want to use one of these techniques, find out more and give it a go!	

Fig. 12. Methods (Links to Activity 2.2.3).

Table 15. Speaking to Others (Links to Activity 2.2.3).

Who are you going to speak to?	How many of these people do you need to speak to?	Which method will you use?	Where will you speak to them?	When will you speak to them?

Table 16. Research Ethics (Links to Activity 2.2.5).

Looking after those who take part in your research....

Planning your research

How will you make sure you approach your research in a fair way and look after anyone who takes part?

Designing your research

Are there any issues in this research that might affect the people you want to speak to (upset them or make them feel uncomfortable)?

Yes   or   No

If yes what will you do about it:

When you deliver your research

Let anyone taking part know:

(1) Who you are

(2) What your research is about

(3) What you will be asking people taking part to do

(4) How you hope to use your research (what are you going to do with it)

(5) That people can choose to take part or not

(6) That you will disguise people's names (you will not use their real name)

(7) That the information of people who take part will only be shared with people in the research team but could be shared with an adult (particularly if you are worried).

(8) Any information gathered will be looked after by the research team.

Remember: if you are worried about anything - speak to an adult!

After your research

- Keep your word (only share the information in the way you said you would)

- Keep all the information you have gathered safe and if you get rid of it - do it carefully so others do not get your information.

2.3 Give It a Go

Workshop Guidance
Aim:

Sometimes, you just have to give something a try.

(1) Doing this in a reflective way (being prepared to review and think through) is always helpful – even if it doesn't work out, how you expect/want. Regardless, it will be a great learning opportunity.

So, when you feel ready – try it out and see how you get on.

Be ready to 'pause' if you need to reflect and review. Remember it's okay for things to change.

Objectives:

Be confident to try out your plans

Resources/Delivery:

This will be defined by the nature of the research ideas you are engaging with.

Make use of the thinking from previous activities – What questions? What methods?

You will need resources relevant to initiatives you have planned.

Activity 2.3.1 – Try It out
Explain: The best thing here is just to give it a go.

Invite: the groups to put into action the method they have identified. Try it out on one another (or if you have a friendly group of people, you can ask to take part – try it out on them).

The key here is to carefully capture the responses you get.

Reflect: How did your chosen method work? What would you do the same and what would you do differently? Make note of your reflections/ observations.

2.4 Keep on Learning

Workshop Guidance

Aim: The final part is to analyse your findings and share them

- 4.1– Reflect and review.

- 4.2 – What have you discovered?

- 4.3 – Have you got an answer to your mini questions/big question - do you need to ask any more questions?

- 4.4 – Share what you have discovered.

Objectives:

- To understand the process for inputting and analysing data.

- To consider how best to share your findings.

- To evaluate your research.

Resources/Delivery:

You will need the data from your previous research activities – the data you have collected.

If you are doing this as a learning exercise, then you can create some data for your team of *Change Makers* to work with.

You may need a computer for this session. This can be used alongside data input and analysis as well as sharing your findings.

Activity 2.4.1 – What Have We Discovered?

Explain: This is our chance to think about what we discovered. Our first step is to get the data ready for us to look at and then we need to look at it and see how it answers our questions.

Invite: each group to look through the data they have collected. Then prepare it for analysis:

(1) Input data.

(2) Analyse that data.

[Have a look at the tips below]

Reflect: What have you discovered?

Note: Tips for inputting and analysing data

There are two main types of research data:

(1) Numbers: for example, how many apples have been eaten?

(2) Stories: for example, how do you feel when you are dancing?

This links to our use of open and closed questions:

- Closed questions create number data

- Open questions create story data

Number data:

To analyse number data, you need to find a way to sort/organise it. You can easily do this using database software (such as excel). Identify:

- What have you counted?

- How have you counted it?

Set up your database to receive this information.

Databases can count the data for you; they can also create charts or tables to display that data and help you think about it.

Once you have answers to your questions then look for:

- Similarities.

- Differences.

Between the numbers you have collected.

For example: your data might show more children eat an apple each day than adults. You can then think about why this is.

Story data:

To analyse story data, you also need to find ways to sort and organise it. To help:

(1) Take all your results – this might be your notes from a focus group

(2) Look at keywords from your results – what stands out?
     (Using our example, people might say that dancing makes them feel 'joyful', 'excited' and 'confident', but they might also say 'unsure' or 'uncertain' if they don't know the dance. Note these different words).

(Continued)

(3) Use the key words to help you identify some themes. For example, (1) dance as fun (2) dance as a learning challenge.

(4) Take your themes and look for similarities and differences across your notes in relation to those themes. For example, note how many talk about dance as fun but also those that don't and the reasons they provide for this.

(5) Use this to then shape your findings, linking it back to the research question you asked.

Learning how to analyse data takes time. But don't be discouraged. Just give it a go. Try out aspects of the guidance above and add to this each time you do a new piece of research.

More guidance on www.learningallowed.org

Activity 2.4.2 – Have You Got an Answer

Invite: Considering the data above, have you got what you need to answer your:

- Mini questions.

- Big question.

Reflect: Do you need to ask any more questions? If so, to whom?

Activity 2.4.3 – Share What You Have Discovered

Explain: It is time to let people know the answers to your questions.

Invite: Think through these questions:

- Who are you going to share it with?

- How will you present your findings to others?
  (write a report/a blog post/a podcast)

Here is a format for presenting your ideas.

(1) Who are you?

(2) What is your research question?

(3) Why did you choose it?

(4) What were your methods?

- How did you ask your questions? – Focus groups/questionnaires?

- Who did you ask them to? How many people?/what questions did you ask?

(5) What did you discover?

(6) What are your conclusions/recommendations?

Have a go at putting a report or output (eg: infographic) together.

Reflect: What worked well as you put your report/output together? What might you change next time? What was the response of people who saw your report/output?

Activity 2.4.4 – Reflect and Review

Explainer: Being a pathfinder is an ongoing journey. One experience adds to the next, which adds to the next, so we need to keep on learning.

Invite: each group to think back through the process:

- What worked well?

- What didn't work so well?

Reflect: What have you learnt about yourself during this process and how can you build on it for next time?

2.5 A Project – Researching Children's Rights

Workshop Guidance

Here is a trial project that allows you to practise some of the skills learnt above. It will, therefore, give you a chance to develop some basic research skills, but importantly, it will help you reflect on children's rights. *Notably,* this activity will help create information sheets that will be of use for Workshop 3 (Chapter 8).

Aim: To help develop the workshops and as a way of practising some of your research skills, develop a series of information sheets to support the next series of workshop activities. See the example below Fig. 13.

(Continued)

You might also find these following fact sheets useful https://right-sofchildren.ca/childrens-rights-under-review/childrens-rights-fact-sheets/

This activity picks up on the theme of children's rights – Chapter 3. It invites the groups to find out a little more about children's rights. To help you explore these themes look at:

- United Nations Convention on the Rights of the Child.

- United Nations Sustainable Development Goals.

- United Nations Convention on the Rights of Persons with Disabilities.

- Declaration on the Rights of Indigenous Peoples.

Themes: Some suggested themes are outlined below

- The Right to be Safe.

- The Right to be Me.

- The Right to Health.

- The Right to Home.

- The Right to Education.

However, you might also consider other themes such as:

- Children and Poverty.

- Child Carers.

- Living with Discrimination.

- Ability and Disability.

- Children and Work.

Objectives:

- Design an information sheet.

- Practise using research skills to understand issues.

- Frame research in a clear and effective way.

Resources/Delivery:

Use the example sheet – Table 10 – to help groups plan their research teams. We have suggested you add a section on *Change Makers*. What can you find to support children's participation in this area:

- See models in Chapter 3.

- Look at international legislation/policy.

To keep your info sheets relevant, think about adding in UN Sustainable Development Goals (UN, 2024). Pick a number of goals (depending on the number of groups you are working with) and consider

- What is the focus of that goal?

- What issue is it trying to solve and how?

- What difference will it make?

Activity 2.5.1 – Researching Children's Rights

Explainer: Your task is to come up with some information sheets on issues impacting children around the world.

Invite:

(1) Pick a theme that you and your group would like to investigate. Here are some examples:

  - The Right to be Safe.

  - The Right to be Me.

  - The Right to Health.

  - The Right to Home.

  - The Right to Education.

(2) Research your theme: once you have a theme use the following headings to help you investigate[…]

  - 'Heading' – what's your topic.

  - 'Case Study' – a story about one child's experience.

  - 'Info' – some interesting information that connects that 'topic' to children's lives.

(Continued)

- 'Facts' – some key facts that catch your attention and make you think.

- 'Rights and Responsibilities' – highlight any relevant sections from the convention.

- UN Sustainable Development Goals – which goal are you focussing on.

- *Change Makers:* find some examples of ways children are engaged as *Change Makers* in this area.
  You will need access to the Internet and some books to help you.

(3) Write up your findings: once you have some information for each theme, pick out the most important – the elements that wow you and interest you and put them into a document.

Reflect: what have you learnt about your research skills from this activity? What worked well and what would you do differently?

Note: we know that in some countries where you might develop a *Change Maker* Club, there are some really important recommendations that relate to enabling Indigenous communities to have a voice. Please explore these as part of your research.

'R' Right to Education

EquippingKids — Research, Create, Inspire

Case Study

Malala always loved going to school and having the opportunity to learn. But...

a group of adults wanted to stop Malala and other girls from going to school - they did not think it was their place.

Malala disagreed.

Aged 11 years old Malala started a blog saying just why her education and that of other girls was so important. Some people didn't like this so one day they stopped the bus she was travelling on to school and shot her. Malala survived and now more than every believes in children's right to the opportunities education provides.

Facts

1 in 4 children around the world are not learning to read and write

168 million children around the world work

1 in every 11 children of primary school age does not go to school

Info

How do you spend your day?

Learning offers a fantastic opportunity. Some children do not get that chance.

Children work making soccer balls, others the trainers children wear to play soccer.

Children make clothes. Children make bricks. Children work in mines. Children work in ...

All these children want to go to school.

Education creates opportunies and gives children the chance to make their own choices

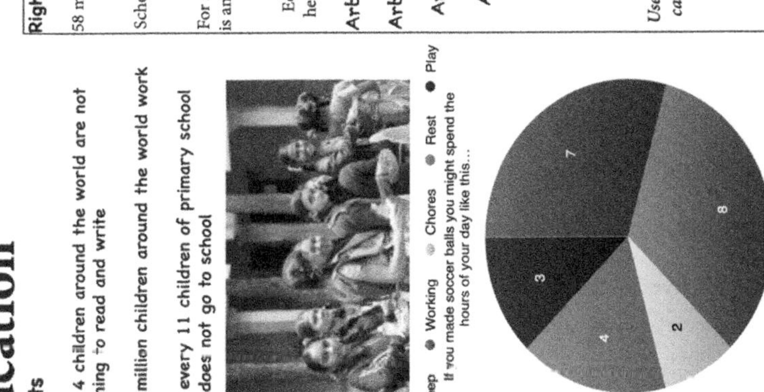

Rights and Responsibilities

58 million children do not even get the chance to go to school!

School is an opportunity that all children should be able to make the most of.

For some school is not allowed to be a priority. This is an adult decision that could have a serious impact on our world.

Education is key to all our futures and is at the heart of the United Nations 2030 gloable targets.

Article 28 All Children have the right to primary education

Article 29 All children have the right to develop their potential through education

Article 38 Children must not be involed in work that exploits them

Articel 15 The right to meet with friends

Find out more:
ilo.org
Malala.orh
stopchildlabour.eu
fairtrade.org.uk

Use your reading skills on the internet to see if you can compare the salary of a sporting hero with a child working in the sports industry.

Fig. 13. Example Information Sheet (Links to Activity 2.5).

Research Ethics – Guidance for Facilitators

Workshop Guidance

Aim:

In this section, we focus on how you as a team of facilitators can build your confidence around talking/discussing ethics.

We suggest you run this session with your fellow facilitators first and then you can think about how you might adapt/use elements of it with your *Change Maker* team.

Ethics is complicated, but it should not stop you from running or delivering a project; you just need to make sure you are paying attention to some key principles and you ensure that you are acting in accordance with any research guidance from any organisation that you are working within/or with.

Objectives:

- To have a greater awareness of ethical issues/questions.

- How you might want to develop a session with children.

Resources/Delivery:

Make use of Appendix A to help you navigate/engage with this content.

Activity 2.5.1

Explain: This session is all about exploring ethical issues/questions that you would want to be aware of if researching with others.

Invite: Facilitators to engage with the following questions:

Question 1: How can you make sure that your project is safe?

Notes: Think through different parts of your project that may pose harm to anyone. Jot down your ideas. From here, think about how you can make your project as safe as possible.

For example: I want to do a project about bullying. I want to do interviews to understand how young people are impacted by bullying. So, I will need to make sure that my questions do not cause the participants to feel stressed or upset. So, I'm going to avoid asking them questions about their direct experiences with bullying. Instead, I am going to make up character names and scenarios where the characters are bullied and then ask the children their thoughts about how the characters were treated and how it may make them feel. I'm also going to make sure that if they do get upset, they can stop the interview at any time and I will make sure there's a trusted adult that can support them.

Reflect on Question 1:

After you've discussed your thoughts, make a list of all of the potential issues that you need to think through. Develop a mini plan for each issue so that you feel prepared to address issues as they come up! Remember the goal is to make sure that participants feel safe and comfortable as they take part in your project.

Question 2: How can you make sure that the information you gather is protected?

Notes: Think about what you are going to do with the information when you collect it. It's important to make sure that you don't share it with others because a lot of this information may be personal. What can you do to protect the information? Jot down your ideas.

For example: Back to the project about bullying. When I do the interviews with children, I will make sure that they are done in a private space where the participants feel comfortable. Any notes that I make I will keep on my laptop and I will use a password to protect the information. Or, I could make hand written notes on what the participants say and keep them in a protected folder. I'll make sure that only myself and my research team have access to these notes. I'm also going to give the participants a fake name; this will help to protect their identity. For example, if one of the children's name's is Rose, I will change her name to Katie and use the name Katie for the rest of my project. This will ensure that anything Rose says doesn't link back to her real name. This is important because some participants may want to keep their ideas safe and may not want anyone else to know what they shared.

Reflect on Question 2:

After you've discussed your thoughts, make a list of all of the ways you can protect your information.

Question 3: Should children decide if they participate in a project or should their parents? Or, should they decide together?

Notes: It's important that children have all of the information they need about the project in order to decide if they want to take part. How will you tell children about the project? What information do they need to know in order to decide if they want to participate? Jot down your ideas.

(Continued)

For example: Back to the project about bullying. Before I do the interviews with children, I need to make sure they understand what the project is about and what it will involve. So, I'm going to give them a fact sheet that has everything about the project they need to know. For example, the fact sheet will outline: the interview will last for one hour, the project is about understanding what children think about bullying, children's names will be protected and if they decide at any time, they do not want to participate they can leave the project without anything bad happening to them.

It is important to make sure you have relevant safeguarding helplines available that can be shared as needed (please check any internal policies your organisations might have).

Reflect on Question 3:
After you've discussed your thoughts, make a list of all the things you need to do to make sure children understand the project and can decide if they want to take part.

For more information contact us www.learningallowed.org

8

BEING AN INFLUENCER – IN PRACTICE

FACILITATOR INTRODUCTION

Be an Influencer	I have a deep awareness and practical 'know how' to communicate and share their knowledge
	I understand different platforms for amplifying a message
	I recognise skills to express, explain and listen to ideas and opinions

The aim of this chapter is to demonstrate the way children can evolve their skills as influencers, by actively applying their communication skills.

Performance:

This chapter is all about building confidence and inviting participants to recognise their skills to communicate a message in a powerful and effective way.

As a result, you might wish to really invest time into developing the artistic outputs (for example a song) from this session into a high-quality performance. This takes time and involves a lot of practice.

The sessions below allow children to test out and explore interests and ideas; you can then invite them to pick one of these artistic outputs to focus on, develop, and to then perform it. The impact of such performances has always been worth the effort!

Making connections to previous content:

The final workshop in Chapter 7, being a pathfinder, was all about creating some information sheets relating to children's rights and their everyday lives. These can be used to support the activities below.

OVERVIEW PLAN

Table 17. Overview Chapter 8 (Set out in Table 17).

Theme/Focus	Workshop	Activities
Being an Influencer	3.1 Your voice matters	3.1.1: Communication skills
	3.2 Using your voice	3.2.1: Speaking out
	3.3 Expressing your ideas	3.3.1: Amplifying your voice
		3.3.2: Say it with music

3.1 – Your Voice Matters

Workshop Guidance
Aim:

The aim of the activity is to examine basic social justice themes, such as fairness, individual voice, non-discrimination, equal opportunities, protection from those with more power and to enable children to realise that they have got skills they can use to respond. For example as 'an influencer', you might enjoy:

- Reading: This can be used to find out information about the issues facing children around the world.

- Arts: Drawing, dance, drama, and music can all be used to raise awareness, either directly through posters or performances or through events.

- Sporting Skills: A great skill for driving a fundraising activity.

- Writing: Let people know about the issues – blog it, send letters, write a poem.

- IT Skills/Maths: Creating platforms and collecting data to share issues.

- Talking: Simply by telling someone else about these stories you can raise awareness and start a journey to make a difference.

Objectives:

- Recognise you have skills to make a difference.

- Understand the role communication plays in supporting change.

Resources/Delivery:
Pen/paper/craft materials

These activities invite children to reflect on the experiences of others. For this, you will either need

- Case study reports (see Figure 10).
  or

- A series of case studies you have found or put together, using books or online sources (for a framework see Figure 10).

If your group of children have created fact sheets from Workshop 2 (Chapter 7), try and encourage them to take one that is not their own. All activities are designed for small groups (about five children).

Activity 3.1.1 – Communication Skills

Explain: This activity will help us to think a little more about what it means to be a *Change Maker* and capabilities or skills we have as communicators.

Invite: each small group to read a fact sheet [see Chapter 7 and notes above] and engage with the questions below:

Question 1: How do hearing these stories make you feel?

Children record their responses.

Question 2: Why do you think you feel like this?

Children record their feelings.

Question 3: So having heard these stories, what do you want to do about it?

Children record their feelings.

Reflect: on the skills children feel they have to respond (see list above in session aims).

- What skills do you have to respond?

- How and in what ways can you be involved in 'influencing' a change, using your communication skills?

(Continued)

Note: The goal here is to remind children that even something as simple as 'talking' about these issues helps to raise awareness and encourages change.

You may wish to roll these two workshops together.

3.2 – Using Your Voice

Workshop Guidance
Aim:

An important part of communicating is realising your voice has value. Here we focus on developing an argument and presenting it. The goal is to build confidence and encourage children to discuss important and sometimes challenging issues.

To bring this workshop to life, we suggest you ask children to imagine they are no longer at their school/youth group but they have been transported to the 'Change Maker Forum of Nations'. Top adult decision-makers from around the world have gathered and have invited the children to represent their voices.

Part A – groups will prepare an argument based on the information sheets.

Part B – groups will then present their arguments one at a time. Give them one minute to present. Argue against their position, then give them 30 seconds to respond.

It works well to pretend that the children are in a formal space. Depending on how many adults are available, you could have a Forum President, A Speaker, to control proceedings, and A Leader, with opposing views to challenge what the children have said.

Objectives:

- grow in confidence.

- develop an argument.

- present their thinking.

- respond to challenges.

Resources/Delivery:

You will need to think about putting children into small groups – four or five children in each.

You will also need paper and pens.

Information sheets (see earlier activities).

You may also want some props to add to the mini drama that the activity encourages.

Activity 3.2.1 – Speaking Out

Explain that the children are no longer at their school/youth group but they have been transported to the Change Maker Forum of Nations. Top adult decision-makers from around the world have gathered, and you have been invited to represent children's voices.

Invite: each group to take one of the issues from the resources sheets from earlier and build an argument. Here is a format to help.

Part A – Prepare Your Arguments

(1) *What is the issue?*
   What are you trying to argue? What key point do you want to make?
   For example: All children have the right to be safe and not to have to fight in wars.

(2) *How does this issue make you feel? Why do you feel like this?*
   Bring the issue to life.
   For example, when I hear about children fighting in wars it makes me feel [...] This was how I felt when I heard about the story of Ishmael[...]

(3) *Support your argument.*
   Use facts and figures to help make your point.
   For example, Ishmael is not the only child impacted by this issue – thousands of children are currently fighting in wars and 449 million are living in warzones.

(4) *Sum up your argument.*
   Remind your listeners of your key points.

(5) *Practise your argument.*
   Your argument should last for no more than one minute [you can increase this as required].

(Continued)

Part B – Present Your Arguments

Explain: you are now in the forum chamber. You will have one minute to present your argument. This will be challenged and then you will have another minute to reply.

Invite: each group to present their ideas, using the format you have created.

Reflect: How was this exercise? What did you learn? What will you remember when you look to create an argument to 'influence' others?

3.3 – Expressing Your Ideas

Workshop Guidance
Aim:

This activity is all about looking at creative ways to influence others as participants recognise how their own interests or skill sets offer a basis to be an influencer.

Here are some creative activities to think about. You can choose one for everyone to work on, or you could leave the children to pick.

- Art: Photography, drawing, craft, pottery, clay, lego, and postcards.

- Film: Use a tablet to create a one min trailer that shares a message.

- Drama: Use freeze frames to explore emotions and reflect on an issue.

- Creative Writing: Come up with your own graphic novel or story.

- Puppet Shows: Mix art and storytelling to communicate a message.

- Music – see 3.3.2

Objectives:

- To recognise creative methods for communicating.

- To understand the power of story.

- To experience the impact of sharing your message.

Resources/Delivery:

This is a really fun workshop all based around storytelling and performance. In the first instance, it is all about getting groups to think through different methods in a fun way. However, these ideas could evolve into a high quality performance piece (see notes on 'performance' at the start of the chapter).

You will need creative materials – pens, papers, craft material and drama props!

Engage in small groups.

Activity 3.3.1 – Amplifying Your Voice

Explain: it is time to be creative in expressing your ideas and influencing others

Invite: children in small groups to

(1) Pick a topic from the fact sheets (see Chapter 7 and earlier in this chapter) that you have been using.
Example: children living in poverty.

(2) On a blank piece of paper explore what stands out to you about this issue?

- What makes you say 'wow'.

- What needs to change?
Come up with three or four key issues that you think others need to hear.
Example: Ashanti lives in a slum in Nairobi Kenya. Key issues:

- It is one of the most densely populated places to live on earth.

- All Ashanti's family share a room.

- 150 people share the same toilet.

(3) Consider if there is any more research you need to do on the issues.

(4) Pick a format to communicate these key issues to influence others and raise their awareness. What will allow you to communicate your message and share the experience of children around these issues?
Here is the list from the introduction

(Continued)

- Art: Photography, drawing, craft, pottery, clay, lego, and postcards.

- Film: Use a tablet to create a 1 min trailer that shares a message.

- Drama: Use freeze frames to explore emotions and reflect on an issue.

- Creative Writing: come up with your own graphic novel or story.

- Puppet Shows: mix art and storytelling to communicate a message.

- Music – see 3.3.2
  Example: a puppet show is a commonly used format for communicating issues around health; this could work well for exploring children and poverty

(5) Groups might like to come up with a story to help them communicate their ideas.
Based around the theme and the facts you have on your information sheet,

- Where is your story set?
  Example: Kenya

- Who are your characters?
  Example: Ashanti and her sister[…]

- How do you imagine what your characters experience?

  – What do they see?

  – What do they feel?

  – What do they hear?

  – What do they smell?

  – What do they taste?

- Write a script - what is the:

  - Beginning of your story – how will you catch people's attention?

  - Middle of your story – what is going to happen and how will it explain the 'key issues'?

  - End of the story – how will your story leave your audience with something to think about?

  - What else will you add to your story to connect with your audience? (Can you make it funny, include props or audience interaction?)
    If you are doing a puppet show, create some puppets to tell your story (this can be done really simply with two dimensional puppets. A face on a stick! You can of course take this further and be more elaborate in your puppet design).

Practice
Perform to your chosen audience (to start with just others in your club)

Reflect: How did your performance go? Use questions like those below to help you review.

What impact did it have? Did people 'hear' your message? What made your message stand out? What would you do the same/differently next time?

Activity 3.3.2 – Say It With Music
Explain: Take some of your key issues and turn this into an awareness raising rap or song.

Invite: groups to

(1) Come up with a four-line rhyming poem. This could be your chorus. Then try and come up with at least one verse – you can then repeat your chorus. The first two lines are always the hardest, so once you have that it is all a lot easier.
Example:
Listen up – make sure you're awake.
A right to education is not a mistake.
Learning gives you choices – it gives control.
Unlocking our voices and potential.
Add a verse

(Continued)

(2) Fit your rhyming poem to a beat or come up with a tune of your own.

You may wish to take a tune you already know and develop their lyrics to fit that. Instrumental versions of many popular songs can be found online (just be careful of any copyright issues).

(3) Rehearsal is key–don't forget that a dance always helps to get the message across.

(4) Perform to your chosen audience.

Reflect: How did your performance go? Use questions like those below to help you review.

What impact did it have? Did people 'hear' your message? What made your message stand out? What would you do the same/differently next time?

9

BEING A CONNECTOR – IN PRACTICE

FACILITATOR INTRODUCTION

Be Connectors	We can recognise our own feelings and the feeling of others
	We can navigate interactions/encounters effectively

Pathfinder skills allow knowledge to be gathered, being an influencer allows knowledge to be shared and being a connector sees the *Change Maker* understand how the process of knowledge creation can be used to make connections that can empower members of a community to be involved in a meaningful process of change.

Whatever part of society we find ourselves in, home, schools and business, research is showing that 'good relationships keep us healthier and happier. Period' (Waldinger & Schulz, 2023, p. 10). It is perhaps not surprising therefore, that we see governments from around the world looking at the ingredients that shape lifelong learning with 'collaboration' being noted as a central skill that governments are seeking to encourage (Skills Development Scotland, 2018). It is not just a focus that enables effective learning but also broader productivity. The result is that businesses are increasingly valuing people who are relationship builders – who are connectors. Fred Kiel's ground breaking study with business leaders showed the value of 'investing' in relationships through promoting integrity, compassion, forgiveness and responsibility (Kiel, 2015).

Here we offer a starting point for how positive relationships can be at the heart of your 'club' as you make visible a capability that enables change makers by bringing people together.

Making connections to previous content:
Here you will want to be looking back on all that we have covered before. The connector is the chance to make those 'connections' to recognise how you can bring the process together in order to benefit members of your community in meaningful ways.

In practice:
There are loads of really fun activities out there to help with relationship building – have a look at them and think what might be valuable for your group (for more guidance visit www.learningallowed.org).

AN OVERVIEW PLAN: SET OUT IN TABLE 18

Table 18. Overview Chapter 9.

Theme/Focus	Workshop	Activities
Being a Connector	4.1 Relationship building	4.1.1: Your emotions
		4.1.2: Chat
		4.1.3: Act
		4.1.4: Repair
		4.1.5: Encourage
	4.2 Understanding others	4.2.1: Being empathetic
		4.2.2: Empathy mapping
	4.3 Planning your project	4.3.1: Framing your project
		4.3.2: Measure and evaluate change

4.1 Relationship Building

Workshop Guidance
Aim: Positive relationships are key to projects focused on change. This series of activities provides a chance for you and your group to think about what those positive relationships are and how to create them.

To help the group explore and remember how to go about framing positive relationships, we introduce the mnemonic C.A.R.E

- Chat,

- Act,

- Repair and

- Encourage.

This has come out of a project with children on creating compassionate communities. C.A.R.E. has provided a focus to frame engagement and maintain a focus on relationships.

Objectives:

- What are the key ingredients for building positive relationships

- Recognise the different elements of C.A.R.E

Resources/Delivery:

These exercises can be managed in whatever way suits your group best. You might even want to run these sessions with your facilitators first before you do it with the children.

Think about using these activities to support members of your group explore the language they use to express and explore their feelings.

Try out different words/images within Activity 4.1.1, giving the group different resources to help them express emotions.

Activity 4.1.1 – Your Emotions

Part 1

Explain: Relationships and relationship building help to support change.

Invite: the group to answer the following questions:

(1) What words can you think of to describe your emotions?
     [invite the group to put each word – with a picture – on a
     separate piece of card].

(2) Put the words in order – what is the most positive feeling at the
     one end to the most negative feeling at the other.
     [you can hang them on a bit of string or put them along the
     floor or tables]

(*Continued*)

Reflect: Placing the emotions should be a challenge. What did you discover about the words you use to express your emotions and feelings?

Part 2

[Using what you have done above]

Invite the children to respond to a series of questions you create by going and standing by the emotion it makes them think of [...]

- Your brothers and sisters receive a present but you don't.

- You finish a puzzle.

- You are left out of a game.

Reflect: What stood out to you from this activity? What emotions do you want to encourage as *Change Makers*?

What emotions might tell you that you or others are feeling like a *Muted Citizen* (left out and with no voice)?

Would it be helpful to spend more time exploring and understanding a language/methods for sharing emotions? If so, try to work on this.

Activity 4.1.2 – Chat

Explain: Building on the last activity, to help ensure that we can create an environment for us all to be *Change Makers*, we are going to explore the idea of C.A.R.E – Chat, Act, Repair and Encourage[1]!

This activity is all about 'chat'.

Invite: small groups to think about the questions below:

- What are the best ways to start a conversation?

- What makes you feel that you would like to be part of a conversation?

- Why is having a conversation with other people so important?

Reflect: The assumptions (the thoughts and ideas we hold) can so easily impact our relationships. A negative assumption might mean that we choose to avoid or limit a particular relationship. Having a conversation can break down those barriers.

- Can you think of any groups that might hold assumptions that limit relationships? For example,

  - The way older people think about children.

  - The way people think about those from different cultures.

  - The way that people think about those who listen to certain music.

- Can you think of examples of when a conversation has changed your mind about someone else?

Activity 4.1.3 – Act

Explain: This activity is about 'Act'. The actions we can take to help build and encourage relationships with those around us.

In the last activity, we thought about how 'chatting' can help to break down barriers. But what else can we do?

Invite: In small groups, answer the questions below (the questions link to activity 4.1.1)

- What 'acts' [something someone might do] makes you/us feel happy?

- What 'acts' [something someone might do] makes you/us feel like you fit in?

- What 'acts' [something someone might do] makes you feel like you/us are a *Change Maker*?

Reflect: What did you discover? What 'acts' seem important for members of your team?

How will you remember to put this into practice?

Activity 4.1.4 – Repair

Explain: Now let's think about 'repair'.

The reality is that we all get it wrong at times, and this impacts our relationships. Here we think about how we might repair those relationships.

Invite: In small groups come up with around three different examples of when a relationship broke down (this might be a personal account or from a story – TV/film).

(Continued)

(1) What needed to happen to make that relationship work again?

(2) Did this act of 'repair' happen?

- If not, why not?

  – How did that leave people feeling?

- If it did – what happened?

  – How did that make people feel?

Reflect: There is lots of research that shows the benefits of putting effort into rebuilding relationships.

Restorative justice is an example of a model that values relationships. It offers a very practical method that can be used in your club, as well as other spaces to help manage social encounters (see Hopkins, 2004 – work on restorative justice in schools).

Activity 4.1.5 – Encourage

Explain: The final part of C.A.R.E. is 'encourage'.

Relationships work well when people feel they are happy, fit in, and are connected as *Change Makers*. To support this, we can encourage each other to put the ideas we have explored into practice. For example, 'well done'.

Invite: Let small groups know they have two mins (or whatever time is appropriate) to come up with as many encouraging words or phrases as they can.

- Compare your list with the other groups.

- Rank your encouraging words and phrases, with what gets used the most at the top.

- Who are you most likely to share your encouraging words or phases with?

- Who is most likely to share these encouraging words and phrases with you? Where is this likely to happen?

Reflect? What can you learn from this? How might the answers from this activity help you think about how you use 'encouragement' in your team?

4.2 Understanding Others

Workshop Guidance
Aim:

Here are a couple of activities focused on understanding others. We use a model called 'empathy mapping' to help structure conversations that will allow the group to see issues from the perspectives of different members of your community.

The 'empathy mapping' model can really develop into a key part of your project planning, helping you to identify

- Who to engage with?

- What that person/groups experiences are?

- What needs/challenges they might face?

- What solutions you can provide?

Empathy mapping is no alternative to actually speaking to certain groups, but it does give you a starting point around which to frame your project.

Objectives:

- Understand what empathy is.

- Be aware of the empathy mapping model and how to use it.

Resources/Delivery:

Create a series of scenarios or case studies in the first person.

> *I am Ishmael - I was 12 years old when soldiers came to my village and took me. They trained me and gave me a gun. They told me I was going to be in their army. Holding a gun made me feel like…*

> *I am Katy and I am 10 years old. I live in a busy city. It is really important for me to have spaces where I can go and run around and play. When I heard that my local park was being shut down I felt…*

Take your time with these activities; you might want to repeat it for different members of the community.

(Continued)

Note: There are lots of examples of empathy mapping online – take a look and see what you can learn.

As always you will need paper and pens for these activities.

Activity 4.2.1

Explain: To make connections, it is important to be able to understand others, to show empathy and to put yourself in their shoes.

Invite:

- Ask members of your group to come and stand in a very large pair of shoes (real shoes if you have them!!).

- Read out one of the scenarios/case studies that you have prepared.

- Ask them how they feel.

Reflect: Why do you think putting yourself in someone else's shoes is valuable?

Activity 4.2.2

Explain: Thinking about how people feel is such an important part of any change making project. Consider the questions below: what can you learn about people in your community?

Understanding them will help you to plan a project to create change.

[You can answer this from the perspective of different members of your community]

Invite: In small groups answer, these questions:

- Who are you putting yourselves in the shoes of?

- What do they need?

- What do they see?

- What do they say?

- What do they hear?

- What do they do?

- What do they think and feel?

  – What are their worries or fears?

  – What makes them happy and allows them to achieve their goals?

Reflect: What can you learn about different members of your community? Who would benefit most from a project to create change? What might this project be? How can you partner with these individuals?

4.3 Planning Your Project

Workshop Guidance

Aim: This activity below offers a framework that pulls together many of the tasks and activities that you will have engaged with throughout the workshops.

As you look at Activity 4.3.1, be prepared to head back to those tasks that you engaged with previously and refresh your memories as you start to look to establish a framework for a new *Change Maker* campaign.

Objectives:

- Recognise the framework,

- Understand the different parts and

- Know how to put it into practice.

Resources/Delivery:

The way you engage with this task will be framed by how you wish to take on a campaign. Is this being conducted by the whole group or small groups with your *Change Maker* Team?

Note with this activity – you may find yourself completing a number of project plans for different phases of your project. So within your broader project plan, you might have a sub plan for different elements such as

- Getting started and finding out more

- Engaging with community members

- Collecting data

- Creating solutions

- Sharing your impact

You will need paper and pens for these activities. Also, think about how and where you can store the plans and evaluations tools that you put together.

(Continued)

Activity 4.3.1 – Framing Your Project

Explain: It is important to have a format to help you structure your project.

Invite: using this framework, come up with some plans for your project

Have an idea:

- What is the change you want to create?

 Talk, Listen and Plan:

- As a team – what do you know about the issue?

- Who else do you need to speak to?

- What else do you need to discover/research?

- What steps can you take to turn your ideas into action?

Give it a Go:

- Start to try out your steps.

Keep on Learning

- Keep asking yourself:

  - What are you discovering?

  - How are you recording the change that happens?

  - Do you need to repeat or change a step?

  - Who might you share what you have discovered with?

Reflect: This is an active plan. Having set out your 'steps' you then need to keep reviewing and reflecting on how you are getting on!!

Activity 4.3.2 – Measure and Evaluate Change

Explain: having some ways to measure change can be really valuable in helping you show others the impact your project has had.

Invite: How can you measure change? Think of some ideas.

 Have a look at the three models below – what's useful? How might you use them?

Model 1:

 Respond to these questions – do this at set stages throughout your project.

(1) Where are you now?

(2) Where have you come from? What's changed or what do you want to see change?

(3) Where are you going? What are your aims and what would you like to see change?

(4) How are you going to get there? What needs to happen to reach your goal?

Model 2:

This is called the ripple model:

(1) What have you done?

(2) How has this impacted on children?

(3) How has this impacted on adults?

(4) How has this impacted your community?

(5) How might this impact other communities?

Model 3:

This is all about goal setting. Use these headings:

- Project Name: What's your project called?

- Your Idea: In one sentence what are you trying to do?

- Objectives: In three bullet points what do you want to achieve?

- Activities: Take your three bullet points and list three activities next to each to show how you can make it happen.

- Milestones: Set a goal next to each activity – this will allow you to review whether you reached your aims.

See the example Table 19.

Reflect:

As you review your project, think about questions like

- How were you able to put your 'capabilities' into practice?

- What skills would you like to work on?

Note: more resources are available on www.learningallowed.org also see Frankel, 2018.

Table 19. Project Set Up.

What's your project called?				
E.g. **New playground**	In one sentence what are you trying to do?			
New playground	**E.g.** **To get some new equipment in our local play park.**	In three bullet points what do you want to achieve?		
New playground	To get some new equipment in our local play park.	**E.g.** **-Find out what people want** **-Raise awareness** **-Engage adults who can make the change happen**	Take your three bullet points and list two or three activities next to each to show how you can make it happen...	
New playground	To get some new equipment in our local play park.	-Find out what people want -Raise awareness -Engage adults who can make the change happen	**E.g.** **-Document what is there already** **-Conduct research with local children**	Next to each activity - set a goal - this will allow you to see if you achieved your aims.
New playground	To get some new equipment in our local play park.	-Find out what people want -Raise awareness -Engage adults who can make the change happen	-Document what is there already -Conduct research with local children	**E.g.** **Research with 20 children** **2 page report sharing our findings**

If you are thinking about contacting and engaging with project partners and want to know

- How to write a letter

- What to include in an email

- How to run a meeting

Get in touch www.learningallowed.org

(also see Chapter 4)

NOTE

1.   C.A.R.E is a framework for supporting relationships that has developed by Learning Allowed from work around well-being and enabling compassionate communities.

10

JUST A STARTING POINT

This book has been about our ambition to make the *Change Maker* visible. We have wanted to show how being a

> *'Change Maker' is a sense of identity.*
>
> *It is a way to think about ourselves as free to access and maximise opportunities that are meaningful in shaping how we view our participation; contributing to positive change(s) in our communities (micro or macro).*

Part 1 gave us the chance to reflect on this definition through looking at some of the academic conversations around children and participation using our three statements:

(1) Our [children and adults] identity as a Change Maker is informed by how connected we feel to the social world around us.

(2) Our sense of identity as a Change Maker has implications for the meaning we attach to our participation.

(3) Our sense of identity as a Change Maker expands with an awareness of our own personal capabilities – freeing us to access and maximise meaningful opportunities.

It has allowed an opportunity to not only review the existing landscape for participation but to also offer some alternatives. As a result, it adds to a 'new paradigm' that challenges both adults and children to rethink what it means to be a participant. This demands that we address social limitations that have been placed around children as *Muted Citizens*, restricting opportunities for children to participate in key social institutions (Chapter 2).

To shift this thinking, it requires an acceptance of the active and fluid way in which identities are shaped and reshaped within the context of an individual's everyday life. As such, we introduced the idea of a 'participatory continuum', which responds to the reality that certain social factors (people, place and purpose) all affect the level of connection we hold, with implications for how we might view our participation. Chapter 3 explored this in relation to existing models for participation. What it illustrated was that there is a value in thinking about participation as messy and therefore more than just the act of taking part in a certain project. Rather, by considering more deeply an individual's sense of who they are (not limited to a particular space, time or task) we can examine what participation and being a participant 'means' in shaping the part we play in our communities.

It was that ambition to increase the visibility of what it means to be a *Change Maker* that fuelled a focus on capabilities in Chapter 4. Challenging our thinking about the nature of opportunities and how these might be maximised in ways that increase children's 'freedom' to make choices is compelling. By breaking down the different attributes that relate to four key capabilities, we hope to have sparked increased access that gives children freedom to maximise opportunities to experience and 'learn' what it means to be a *Change Maker*.

Indeed, Part 2 was set up to demonstrate how this could then be applied in practice. For us, it felt exciting to be able to provide a basis that would allow others to think about how the *Change Maker* could be brought to life.

Our challenge to you is to be enthused, creative and ambitious in joining us in taking that first step to make the *Change Maker* visible.

At a time when the world faces so many challenges, a project to unlock children as *Change Makers* offers hope. It has the potential to release a positive force that can bring about change in homes, schools, community spaces and beyond.

This book has been about letting children know, through you, that they can be a *Change Maker*: that it is a 'thing' and that it applies to them! Through making the *Change Maker* visible, we hope that children increasingly find ways to 'do' participation and 'display' themselves as participants (as they wish).[1] The act of participating, we believe, creates possibilities that bring communities together through the shaping of a shared goal or vision. In Chapter 1, it was suggested that a response to local and global challenges requires a unity of thought - a commitment to a 'common good'. Children as *Change Makers* must, therefore, be part of the solution.

We hope that what we have shared in the previous pages offers a starting point. However, we remain committed to learning alongside you as you breathe life into the *Change Maker* and inspire children to recognise an identity that has the power to be truly transformational.

To stay involved in this conversation, join us on www.learningallowed.org

NOTE

1.   Research from the family (Finch, 2007) highlighted how 'doing' certain things helped to build bonds within a family. Here, we are inviting a consideration of how a certain presentation of self as a participant might strengthen and further community bonds.

APPENDICES

APPENDIX A: RESEARCH ETHICS CONSIDERATIONS

Navigating ethical issues and considerations can be tricky. As a result, we have developed a section for research facilitators that focuses on research ethics. We have included activities below, so you can think about research ethics and prepare accordingly in advance of carrying out activities on research ethics with children. Prior to starting any activities, we suggest that facilitators complete ethics training. You can check out fhi 360 Research Ethics Training Curriculum (RETC), Second Edition as a starting point.

For any Canadian facilitators, for example, you can check out the Tri-Council Policy Statement: Ethical Conduct for Research Involving Humans (TCPS 2) training on research ethics (don't forget to save your certificates!):

https://tcps2core.ca/welcome

The training is organised in modules and reviews key ethical issues pertaining to research with human participants.

Here are some ethics activities that you can carry out with facilitators:

Use the following visuals as a guide and get everyone to think about challenges associated with each topic. Start by reviewing the info in each box and then ask the following discussion question: What challenges are associated with….

Privacy and Confidentiality

> Respecting the privacy and confidentiality of children participating in research involves close consideration of several aspects, including: privacy with regard to how much information the child wants to reveal or share, and with whom; privacy in the processes of information gathering/data collection and storage that allows the exchange of information to be confidential to those involved; and privacy of the research participants so that they are not identifiable in the publication and dissemination of findings.

*Derived from Ethical Research Involving Children (2024).

Harms and Benefits

> The most fundamental consideration in undertaking research involving children is deciding whether the research actually needs to be done, if children need to be involved in it, and in what capacity. Accordingly, at the very outset of the research process researchers need to engage with critical issues regarding the purpose of the research and the impact that participating in the research may have on children in terms of potential harms and possible benefits.

*Derived from Ethical Research Involving Children (2024).

Informed Consent

> Obtaining consent from parents/carers and children is central to the research relationship and signals respect for the research participant's dignity, their capability to express their views and their right to have these heard in matters that affect them. Informed consent is an explicit agreement which requires participants to be informed about, and have an understanding of, the research. This must be given voluntarily and be renegotiable, so that children may withdraw at any stage of the research process.

*Derived from Ethical Research Involving Children (2024).

Payment and Compensation

> Research participants should be appropriately reimbursed for any expenses, compensated for effort, time or lost income, and acknowledged for their contribution. Payment should be avoided if it potentially pressures, coerces, bribes, persuades, controls, or causes economic or social disadvantage. The guiding principles of justice, benefit and respect underpin the need for research participants to be properly acknowledged, adequately recompensed and given fair returns for their involvement.

*Derived from Ethical Research Involving Children (2024).

Explain some of the key issues associated with these ethical topics. For example:

(1) Privacy and Confidentiality

Challenges:

- Disclosure of critical information/duty to report.
- Confidentiality from parent(s)/caregivers.
- Privacy from adults/parent(s)/caregivers.
- Sharing findings.

(2) Harms and Benefits

Challenges:

- Dominant perception(s) of children as incompetent/over-protection.
- University Research Ethics Boards.
- Providing spaces for children's voices.
- Discussing sensitive information/subjects.
- Support during/after research process.

(3) Informed Consent

Challenges:

- Consent is based on the notion of 'capacity/competency'.
- Obtaining consent from children/informed consent from parents.
- To consent = let something happen (permission for something to occur).

(4) Payment and Compensation

Challenges:

- Determining the nature of payment in various contexts.
- Payment may impact family/community dynamics.
- Challenges surrounding unrealistic expectations.
- Power dynamic between researcher and researched.

After these discussions, get the groups to review the following case studies below and ask them to think about the questions in relation to case studies on each of these areas:

- Identify the ethical challenge(s) the researcher(s) experienced.
- Reflect on the choices made and whether you think this was the right choice or if you would have made a different choice.
- Why are these challenges/choices important and why do they matter?

Case Studies to Use While Reflecting on These Questions

(1) Privacy and Confidentiality

Case study: https://childethics.com/case-studies/interviewing-children-with-disability-in-the-presence-of-a-parent-by-berni-kelly/

(2) Harms and Benefits

Case study: https://childethics.com/case-studies/finding-the-balance-between-protection-and-participation-what-do-you-do-when-follow-up-services-are-not-readily-available-by-monica-ruiz-casares/

(3) Informed Consent

Case study: https://childethics.com/case-studies/addressing-issues-of-consent-and-participation-in-research-with-young-people-by-paulina-billett/

(4) Payment and Compensation

Case study: https://childethics.com/case-studies/__trashed/

Note that there are multiple other case studies focusing on these topics that are accessible at the following link:

https://childethics.com/resources/case-studies/

Work through a few of these case studies and get the groups to discuss key ethical issues and decisions.

Next, it's time for your groups to think about how they will manage some of these ethical issues. Working in groups, get them to reflect on the following questions for each topic:

(1) *Privacy and confidentiality*

How will you protect your participants' privacy? How will you ensure that the data remain confidential?

(2) *Harms and Benefits*

Will there be any harm associated with your project? If so, outline how this will be mitigated. What are the benefits of children's participation?

(3) *Informed Consent*

How will you ensure informed consent? Do parents need to be involved?

(4) *Payment and Compensation*

Will you provide compensation? If so, what will it be? Is it appropriate to your participant demographic? How will you get the compensation to your participants?

For more information on research ethics, check out https://childethics.com/

REFERENCES

Adorjan, M., & Ricciardelli, R. (2019). A new privacy paradox? Youth agentic practices of privacy management despite "nothing to hide" online. *The Canadian Review of Sociology, 56*(1), 8–29. https://doi.org/10.1111/cars.12227

Alderson, P. (2017). Utopian research with children. In P. M. Christensen & A. James (Eds.), *Research with children: Perspectives and practices* (3rd ed.). Routledge. https://doi.org/10.4324/9781315657349

Alexander, J., & Conrad, A. (2022). *Citizens, Kingston upon Thames.* Canbury Publishing.

Arnstein, S. (1969). A ladder of citizenship participation. *Journal of the American Institute of Planners, 35*(4), 216–224.

Bacon, K., & Frankel, S. (2014). Rethinking children's citizenship, negotiating structure, shaping meanings. *The International Journal of Children's Rights, 22*(1), 21–42. https://doi.org/10.1163/15718182-55680003

Brake, M. (1980). *The sociology of youth culture and youth subculture.* Routledge and Kegan Paul.

Brooks, L. (2003). *Kid power.* The Guardian.

Christensen, P. M., & James, A. (2017). Researching children and childhood: Cultures of communication. In P. Christensen & A. James (Eds.), *Research with children: Perspectives and practices* (3rd ed.). Routledge. https://doi.org/10.4324/9781315657349

Cohen, S. (1999). Moral panics and folk concepts. *Paedagogica Historica, 35*(3), 585–591. https://doi.org/10.1080/0030923990350302

Cordero Acre, M. (2012). Towards an emancipatory discourse of children's rights. *The International Journal of Children's Rights, 20*(3), 365–421. https://doi.org/10.1163/157181812X637127

Corsaro, W. (2017). *The sociology of childhood.* Sage Publications.

Cote, J. (1994). *Adolescent storm and stress*. Erlbaum Associates.

Cottam, H. (2018). *Radical help: How we can remake the relationships between us and revolutionise the welfare state*. Virago Press.

Cummings, S. (2020). *Children's voices in politics*. Peter Lang Ltd, International Academic Publishers.

Cunningham, H. (2006). *The invention of childhood*. BBC.

Cunningham, S., & Lavalette, M. (2004). 'Active citizens' or 'irresponsible truants'? School student strikes against the war. *Critical Social Policy*, 24(2), 255–269. https://doi.org/10.1177/0261018304042002

Cussianovich, A. (2001). "What does protagonism mean?" In L. Manfred, O. Bernd, & R. Albert (Eds.), *Working children's protagonism: Social movements and empowerment in Latin America, Africa, and India*. IKO.

Dewey, J. (2011). *Democracy and education*. Simon and Brown.

Doek, J. (2009). The CRC 20 years: An overview of some of the major achievements and remaining challenges. *Child Abuse & Neglect*, 33(11), 771–782. https://doi.org/10.1016/j.chiabu.2009.08.006

Durkheim, E., & Lukes, S. (1982). *The rules of sociological methods: And selected texts on sociology and its methods*. Macmillan.

Ennew, J. (2000). The history of children's rights: Whose story? *Cultural Survival Quarterly*, 42(2), 1–44.

Fass, P. (2011). A historical context for the United Nations convention on the rights of the child. *The Annals of the American Academy of Political and Social Science*, 633(1), 17–29. https://doi.org/10.1177/0002716210382388

Finch, J. (2007). Displaying families. *Sociology*, 41(1), 65–81. https://doi.org/10.1177/0038038507072284

Friere, P. (1970). *Pedagogy of the oppressed*. Seabury Press.

Frankel, S. (2017). *Negotiating childhoods: Applying a moral filter to children's everyday lives* (1st ed.). Palgrave Macmillan. https://doi.org/10.1057/978-1-137-32349-1

Frankel, S. (2018). *Giving children a voice: A step-by-step guide to promoting child-centred practice*. Jessica Kingsley Publishers.

Frankel, S. (2023a). *Establishing child centred practice in a changing world. Part A* (1st ed.). Emerald Publishing Limited.

Frankel, S. (2023b). *Establishing child centred practice in a changing world. Part B*. Emerald Publishing Limited.

Frankel, S., & Whalley, C. (2023). *Learning allowed: Children, communities and lifelong learning in a changing world*. Emerald Publishing Limited.

Freeman, M. (2007). Why it remains important to take children's rights seriously. *The International Journal of Children's Rights, 15*(1), 5–23. https://doi.org/10.1163/092755607X181711

Freire, P. (1970). *Pedagogy of the oppressed*. Continuum.

Gal, T., & Duramy, B. (2015). *International perspectives and empirical findings on child participation: From social exclusion to child-inclusive policies* (1st ed.). Oxford University Press.

Gatto, J. (2005). *Dumbing us down: The hidden curriculum of compulsory schooling*. New Society Publishers.

George, A. (2021). *Make it happen: How to be an activist*. Harpercollins Publishers.

Gooch, G. (2023). Youth political participation in the Canadian Senate. In S. Frankel (Ed.), *Establishing child centred practice in a changing world. Part B*. Emerald Publishing Limited.

Hanson, K., & Vandaele, A. (2003). Working children and international labour law: A critical analysis. *The International Journal of Children's Rights, 11*(1), 73–146. https://doi.org/10.1163/092755603322384038

Hart, R. (1992). *Children's participation: From tokenism to citizenship*. UNICEF International Child Development Centre.

Hattie, J. (2009). *Visible learning: A synthesis of meta learning relating to achievement*. Routledge.

Hopkins, B. (2004). *Just schools: A whole school approach to restorative justice*. Jessica Kinglsey Publishers.

James, A. (1993). *Childhood identities: Self and social relationships in the experience of the child*. Edinburgh University Press.

James, A. (2013). *Socialising children*. Palgrave Macmillan.

James, A., & Prout, A. (1990). *Constructing and reconstructing childhood: New directions in the sociological study of childhood*. Falmer Press.

Jans, M. (2004). Children as citizens: Towards a contemporary notion of child participation. *Childhood (Copenhagen, Denmark)*, *11*(1), 27–44. https://doi.org/10.1177/0907568204040182

Jenkins, R. (2004). *Social identity* (4th ed.). Routledge.

Kennan, D., Brady, B., & Forkan, C. (2018). Supporting children's participation in decision making: A systematic literature review exploring the effectiveness of participatory processes. *The British Journal of Social Work*, *48*(7), 1985–2002. https://doi.org/10.1093/bjsw/bcx142

Kellett, M. (2009). Children and young people's participation. In H. Montgomery, K. Heather, & M. Kellett (Eds.), *Children and young people's worlds: Developing frameworks for integrated practice*. Policy press.

Key, E. (1909 [1900]). *The century of the child*. G.P. Putnam's Sons.

Kiel, F. (2015). *Return on character: The real reason leaders and their companies win*. Harvard Business Review Press.

Kirby, P., & Gibbs, S. (2006). Facilitating participation: Adults' caring support roles within child-to-child projects in schools and after-school settings. *Children & Society*, *20*(3), 209–222. https://doi.org/10.1002/CHI.87

Kitzinger, J. (1997). Who are you kidding? Children power and the fight against sexual abuse. In A. James & A. Prout (Eds.), *Constructing and reconstructing childhood*. Routledge Falmer.

Kohn, A. (2011). *Feel-bad education: And other contrarian essays on children and schooling*. Beacon Press.

Kuhn, T. (1962). *The structure of scientific revolutions*. The University of Chicago Press.

Lansdown, G. (2014). 25 years of UNCRC: Lessons learned in children's participation. *Canadian Journal of Children's Rights*, *1*(1). https://doi.org/10.22215/cjcr.v1i1.12

Larkins, C. (2023). Deeping the roots of children's participation. *Sociedad e Infancias*, *7*(1), 147–163. https://doi.org/10.5209/soci.88645

Leonard, J. (2013). *Principles of social change*. Oxford University Press.

Levitas, R. (2005). *The inclusive society? Social exclusion and new labour* (2nd ed.). Palgrave Macmillan.

Liebel, M. (2008). *Child led research with working children presented in symposium 'working with young researchers' at conference. Child and youth research in the 21st century: A critical appraisal*. International Childhood and Youth Research.

Lundy, L. (2007). "Voice" is not enough: Conceptualising article 12 of the United Nations convention on the rights of the child. *British Educational Research Journal, 33*(6), 927–942. https://doi.org/10.1080/01411920701657033

Lundy, L. (2018). In defence of tokenism? Implementing children's right to participate in collective decision-making. *Childhood (Copenhagen, Denmark), 25*(3), 340–354. https://doi.org/10.1177/0907568218777729

Mackay, D. (1973). Aspects of the theory of comprehension, memory and attention. *The Quarterly Journal of Experimental Psychology, 25*(1), 22–40. https://doi.org/10.1080/14640747308400320

Marshall, T. H. (1995). *Citizenship and social class.* Pluto Press.

Marshall, D. (1999). The construction of children as an object of international relations: The declaration of children's rights and the child welfare committee of league of nations, 1900–1924. *The International Journal of Children's Rights, 7*(2), 103–148. https://doi.org/10.1163/15718189920494309

McCafferty, P. (2017). Implementing article 12 of the United Nations convention on the rights of the child in child protection decision-making: A critical analysis of the challenges and opportunities for social work. *Child Care in Practice: Northern Ireland Journal of Multi-Disciplinary Child Care Practice, 23*(4), 327–341. https://doi.org/10.1080/13575279.2016.1264368

McManus, I. C., Freegard, M., Moore, J., & Rawles, R. (2010). Science in the making: Right hand, heft hand. II: The duck–rabbit figure. *Laterality. 15*(1–2): 166–185. https://doi.org/10.1080/13576500802564266

McNamee, S. (2016). *The social study of childhood: An introduction.* Palgrave Macmillan.

McRobbie, A. (1994). *Postmodernism and popular culture.* Routledge.

Meintjes, H. (2014). Growing up in time of AIDS: The shinning recorders of Zisize. In K. Tisdall, A. Gadda, & U. Butler (Eds.), *Children and young people's participation and its transformative potential.* Palgrave Macmillan.

Mountford, M., & Vento, F. (2023). Children as change maker: Exploring children's meaningful participation in participatory action research through a project on helicopter parenting. In S. Frankel (Ed.), *Establishing child centred practice in a changing world. Part A.* Emerald Publishing Limited.

Muncie, J. (2015). *Youth & crime* (4th ed.). SAGE.

O'Sullivan, J. M. (2021). *An exploration of the barriers and enablers of children's lived participation within the primary school context*. PhD Thesis, University College Cork.

O'Sullivan, J. M., Horgan, D., & O'Riordan, J. (2023). There was no fence. In B. Percy-Smith & B. Percy-Smith (Eds.), *Handbook of children and young people's participation: Conversations for transformational change*. Routledge. https://doi.org/10.4324/9781003367758

Pare, M. (2017). Children's rights are human rights and why Canadian implementation lags behind. *Canadian Journal of Children's Rights*, 4(1), 24–47. https://doi.org/10.22215/cjcr.v4i1.1163

Parsons, T. (1951). *The social system*. Routledge and Regan Paul.

Pearson, G. (1983). *Hooligan: A history of respectable fears*. Macmillan.

Percy-Smith, B., & Thomas, N. (2010). *A handbook of children and young people's participation: Perspectives from theory and practice*. Routledge.

Percy-Smith, B. (2018). Participation as learning for change in everyday spaces: Enhancing meaning and effectiveness using action research. In: C. Baraldi, & T. Cockburn (Eds.), *Theorising childhood*. Studies in childhood and youth. Palgrave Macmillan.

Percy-Smith, B., Thomas, N., O'Kane, C., & Twum-Danso Imoh, A. (2023). *A handbook of children and young people's participation: Conversations for transformational change*. Routledge.

Polonko, K., & Lombardo, L. (2015). Non-governmental organisations and the UN convention on the rights of the child. *The International Journal of Children's Rights*, 23(1), 133–153. https://doi.org/10.1163/15718182-0230100

Reynaert, D., Bouverne-de-Bie, M., & Vandevelde, S. (2009). A review of children's rights literature since the adoption of the United Nations convention on the rights of the child. *Childhood (Copenhagen, Denmark)*, 16(4), 518–534. https://doi.org/10.1177/0907568209344270

Robinson, K. (2006, February). Do schools kill creativity? [Video]. Ted Conferences. https://www.ted.com/talks/sir_ken_robinson_do_schools_kill_creativity?language=en

Robinson, K. (2010, February). Bring on the learning revolution [Video]. Ted Conferences. https://www.ted.com/talks/sir_ken_robinson_bring_on_the_revolution?language=en

Sandel, M. (2010). *Justice: What's the right thing to do?* Farrar, Straus and Giroux.

Sen, A. (1999). *Development as freedom.* Oxford University Press.

Shakespeare, W. (1970). *The winter's tale.* Birham Books.

Shier, H. (2001). Pathways to participation: Openings, opportunities and obligations. *Children & Society, 15*(2), 107–117. https://doi.org/10.1002/chi.617

Shier, H., Mendez, M., Padilla, M., Villlagra, R., Gonalez, P., Valdivia, O., & Torres, N. (2023). *A handbook of children and young people's participation* (2nd ed.). Routledge.

Skills Development Scotland. (2018). *Skills 4.0: A skills model to drive Scotland's future – Skills development Scotland.* https://www.skillsdevelopmentscotland.co.uk/media/44684/skills-40_a-skills-model.pdf

Spencer, G., & Thompson, J. (2023). Reproducing power asymmetries through voice, collaboration and change. In S. Frankel (Ed.), *Establishing child centred practice – Part A.* Emerald Publishing Limited.

Squires, P. (2008). *ASBO nation.* Bristol University Press.

Sticca, F., & Perren, S. (2013). Is cyberbullying worse than traditional bullying? Examining the differential roles of medium, publicity, and anonymity for the perceived severity of bullying. *Journal of Youth and Adolescence, 42*(5), 739–750. https://doi.org/10.1007/s10964-012-9867-3

Stoeckline, D. (2013). Theories of action in the field of child participation: In search of explicit frameworks. *Sage Journals, 20*(4). https://doi.org/10.1177/0907568212466901

Taft, J. (2019). *The kids are in charge: Activism and power in Peru's movement of working children.* NYU Press.

The Canadian Encyclopedia. (2020). https://www.thecanadianencyclopedia.ca/en/article/shannen-koostachin

Thomas, N. (2017). Turning the tables: Children as researchers. In P. Christensen & A. James (Eds.), *Research with children: Perspectives and practices* (3rd ed.). Routledge. https://doi.org/10.4324/9781315657349

Thomas, N., & Stoecklin, D. (2018). Recognition and capability: A new way to understand how children can achieve their rights? In C. Baraldi & T. Cockburn (Eds.), *Theorising childhood: Citizenship, rights and participation*. Palgrave Macmillan.

Thorne, B. (2009). "Childhood": Changing and dissonant meanings. *International Journal of Learning and Media, 1*(1), 19–27. https://doi.org/10.1162/ijlm.2009.00010

Tisdall, K. (2008). Is the honeymoon over? Children and young people's participation in public decision making. *The International Journal of Children's Rights, 16*(3), 343–354.

Tisdall, K., Gadda, A., & Mandel Butler, U. (2014). *Children and young people's participation and its transformative potential*. Palgrave Macmillan.

UN News. (2024). Determination and compromise needed 'for the common good'. https://soundcloud.com/unradio/determination-and-compromise-needed-for-the-common-good-guterres

United Nations. (1989). *Convention on the rights of the child*. United Nations General Assembly.

United Nations. (2024). *Department of economic and social affairs sustainable development*. https://sdgs.un.org/goals

Vickery, J. (2017). *Worried about the wrong things: Youth, risk and opportunity in the digital world*. MIT Press.

Waldinger, R. J., & Schulz, M. S. (2023). *The good life: Lessons from the world's longest scientific study of happiness*. Simon & Schuster.

Wall, J. (2021). *Give children the vote: On democratizing democracy*. Bloomsbury Academic.

Watkins, C., Carnell, E., Lodge, C., Wagner, P., & Whalley, C. (2000). *Learning about learning: Resources for supporting effective learning*. Routledge.

White, S. C. (1996). Depoliticising development: The uses and abuses of participation. *Development in Practice, 6*(1), 6–15. https://doi.org/10.1080/0961452961000157564

Wyness, M. (2013). Children's participation and intergenerational dialogue: Bringing adults back into the analysis. *Childhood (Copenhagen, Denmark), 20*(4), 429–442. https://doi.org/10.1177/0907568212459775

Wyness, M. G. (2019). *Childhood and society/Michael Wyness* (3rd ed.). Red Globe Press/Macmillan International.

INDEX

Printed and bound by CPI Group (UK) Ltd, Croydon, CR0 4YY

25/08/2025

14724058-0002